ACPL ITEM
DISCARDED

Y0-BTD-331

338.47004 Ev6

Evolving the high
performance computing and
communications initiative..

Evolving the High Performance Computing and Communications Initiative to Support the Nation's Information Infrastructure

Committee to Study High Performance Computing and Communications:
Status of a Major Initiative

Computer Science and Telecommunications Board

Commission on Physical Sciences, Mathematics, and Applications

National Research Council

NATIONAL ACADEMY PRESS
Washington, D.C. 1995

NOTICE: The project that is the subject of this report was approved by the Governing Board of the National Research Council, whose members are drawn from the councils of the National Academy of Sciences, the National Academy of Engineering, and the Institute of Medicine. The members of the committee responsible for the report were chosen for their special competences and with regard for appropriate balance.

This report has been reviewed by a group other than the authors according to procedures approved by a Report Review Committee consisting of members of the National Academy of Sciences, the National Academy of Engineering, and the Institute of Medicine.

The National Academy of Sciences is a private, nonprofit, self-perpetuating society of distinguished scholars engaged in scientific and engineering research, dedicated to the furtherance of science and technology and to their use for the general welfare. Upon the authority of the charter granted to it by the Congress in 1863, the Academy has a mandate that requires it to advise the federal government on scientific and technical matters. Dr. Bruce Alberts is president of the National Academy of Sciences.

The National Academy of Engineering was established in 1964, under the charter of the National Academy of Sciences, as a parallel organization of outstanding engineers. It is autonomous in its administration and in the selection of its members, sharing with the National Academy of Sciences the responsibility for advising the federal government. The National Academy of Engineering also sponsors engineering programs aimed at meeting national needs, encourages education and research, and recognizes the superior achievements of engineers. Dr. Robert M. White is president of the National Academy of Engineering.

The Institute of Medicine was established in 1970 by the National Academy of Sciences to secure the services of eminent members of appropriate professions in the examination of policy matters pertaining to the health of the public. The Institute acts under the responsibility given to the National Academy of Sciences by its congressional charter to be an adviser to the federal government and, upon its own initiative, to identify issues of medical care, research, and education. Dr. Kenneth I. Shine is president of the Institute of Medicine.

The National Research Council was organized by the National Academy of Sciences in 1916 to associate the broad community of science and technology with the Academy's purposes of furthering knowledge and advising the federal government. Functioning in accordance with general policies determined by the Academy, the Council has become the principal operating agency of both the National Academy of Sciences and the National Academy of Engineering in providing services to the government, the public, and the scientific and engineering communities. The Council is administered jointly by both Academies and the Institute of Medicine. Dr. Bruce Alberts and Dr. Robert M. White are chairman and vice chairman, respectively, of the National Research Council.

Support for this project was provided by the U.S. Department of Defense through the Advanced Research Projects Agency under Grant No. MDA972-94-1-0008. Any opinions, findings, conclusions, or recommendations expressed in this material are those of the authors and do not necessarily reflect the views of the Department of Defense or the Advanced Research Projects Agency.

Library of Congress Catalog Card Number 95-67707
International Standard Book Number 0-309-05277-7

Copyright 1995 by the National Academy of Sciences. All rights reserved.

Available from:

National Academy Press
2101 Constitution Avenue, NW
Washington, DC 20418

B-540

Printed in the United States of America

COMMITTEE TO STUDY HIGH PERFORMANCE COMPUTING AND COMMUNICATIONS: STATUS OF A MAJOR INITIATIVE

FREDERICK P. BROOKS, JR., University of North Carolina at Chapel Hill, *Co-chair*
IVAN E. SUTHERLAND, Sun Microsystems Laboratories, *Co-chair*
ERICH BLOCH, Council on Competitiveness
DEBORAH ESTRIN, University of Southern California/Information Sciences Institute
JOHN HENNESSY, Stanford University
BUTLER W. LAMPSON, Digital Equipment Corporation
EDWARD D. LAZOWSKA, University of Washington
WILLIAM A. LESTER, JR., University of California at Berkeley
JANE PRESTON, Telemedical Interactive Consultative Services Inc.
W. DAVID SINCOSKIE, Bell Communications Research Inc.
LARRY SMARR, National Center for Supercomputing Applications/University of Illinois at Urbana-Champaign
JOSEPH F. TRAUB, Columbia University

Staff

MARJORY S. BLUMENTHAL, Director
JAMES E. MALLORY, Staff Officer
LESLIE M. WADE, Project Assistant

COMPUTER SCIENCE AND TELECOMMUNICATIONS BOARD

WILLIAM WULF, University of Virginia, *Chair*
FRANCES ALLEN, IBM T.J. Watson Research Center
JEFF DOZIER, University of California at Santa Barbara
DAVID J. FARBER, University of Pennsylvania
HENRY FUCHS, University of North Carolina
CHARLES M. GESCHKE, Adobe Systems Inc.
JAMES GRAY, San Francisco, California
BARBARA J. GROSZ, Harvard University
DEBORAH A. JOSEPH, University of Wisconsin
RICHARD M. KARP, University of California at Berkeley
BUTLER W. LAMPSON, Digital Equipment Corporation
BARBARA H. LISKOV, Massachusetts Institute of Technology
JOHN MAJOR, Motorola Inc.
ROBERT L. MARTIN, AT&T Network Systems
DAVID G. MESSERSCHMITT, University of California at Berkeley
WILLIAM H. PRESS, Harvard University
CHARLES L. SEITZ, Myricom Inc.
EDWARD SHORTLIFFE, Stanford University School of Medicine
CASMIR S. SKRZYPCZAK, NYNEX Corporation
LESLIE L. VADASZ, Intel Corporation

MARJORY S. BLUMENTHAL, Director
LOUISE A. ARNHEIM, Senior Staff Officer
HERBERT S. LIN, Senior Staff Officer
JAMES E. MALLORY, Staff Officer
RENEE A. HAWKINS, Staff Associate
JOHN M. GODFREY, Research Associate
GLORIA P. BEMAH, Administrative Assistant
LESLIE M. WADE, Project Assistant

COMMISSION ON PHYSICAL SCIENCES, MATHEMATICS, AND APPLICATIONS

RICHARD N. ZARE, Stanford University, *Chair*
RICHARD S. NICHOLSON, American Association for the Advancement of Science, *Vice Chair*
STEPHEN L. ADLER, Institute for Advanced Study
SYLVIA T. CEYER, Massachusetts Institute of Technology
SUSAN L. GRAHAM, University of California at Berkeley
ROBERT J. HERMANN, United Technologies Corporation
RHONDA J. HUGHES, Bryn Mawr College
SHIRLEY A. JACKSON, Rutgers University
KENNETH I. KELLERMANN, National Radio Astronomy Observatory
HANS MARK, University of Texas at Austin
THOMAS A. PRINCE, California Institute of Technology
JEROME SACKS, National Institute of Statistical Sciences
L.E. SCRIVEN, University of Minnesota
A. RICHARD SEEBASS III, University of Colorado
LEON T. SILVER, California Institute of Technology
CHARLES P. SLICHTER, University of Illinois at Urbana-Champaign
ALVIN W. TRIVELPIECE, Oak Ridge National Laboratory
SHMUEL WINOGRAD, IBM T.J. Watson Research Center
CHARLES A. ZRAKET, MITRE Corporation (retired)

NORMAN METZGER, Executive Director

Preface

In early 1994, acting through the Defense Authorization Act for FY 1994 (Public Law 103-160), Congress asked the National Research Council (NRC) to examine the status of the High Performance Computing and Communications Initiative (HPCCI). Broad-based interest in and support for the HPCCI exist. Given its scope and size, concerns had been raised about its goals, management, and progress. Congress asked that at a minimum the study address:

- The basic underlying rationale(s) for the program, including the appropriate balance between federal efforts and private-sector efforts;
- The appropriateness of its goals and directions;
- The balance between various elements of the program;
- The effectiveness of the mechanisms for obtaining the views of industry and users for the planning and implementation of the program;
- The likelihood that the various goals of the program will be achieved;
- The management and coordination of the program; and
- The relationship of the program to other federal support of high-performance computing and communications, including acquisition of high-performance computers by federal departments and agencies in support of the mission needs of these departments and agencies.

For this study the NRC's Computer Science and Telecommunications Board (CSTB) convened a committee of 12 members, expert on pioneering applications of computers and communications and the major components of the HPCCI: High-Performance Computing Systems, Advanced Software Technology and Algorithms, the National Research and Education Network, Basic Research and Human Resources, and Information Infrastructure Technology and Applications. Congress asked the committee to accelerate the normal NRC study process in order to provide an interim report by July 1, 1994, and a final report by February 1, 1995. The committee was able to meet this rapid turnaround by drawing on the knowledge and experience of its members as expressed in committee deliberations and by obtaining input from numerous outside experts.

The full committee met six times between March 10, 1994, and December 20, 1994, to hear more than 25 high-performance computing and communications users, builders, and scientists; to discuss the HPCCI in detail; and to produce this report. Additionally, smaller groups of committee members made site visits to discuss first-hand the use of high-performance technologies. These visits involved another 6 individuals from the Ford Motor Company and approximately 50 high-performance computing and communications users who had gathered at a workshop to discuss the use of high-performance systems in environmental research and simulation. In addition to examining the current status of the program, the committee considered the evolution of the HPCCI and its goals and alternate government investment strategies related to technological development. The committee took into account varying perspectives on the initiative's goals and available assessments of progress toward achieving them.

The committee's interim report provided technical background and perspective on the overall development of high-performance computing and communications systems, as well as on the HPCCI, formally started in 1991.[1] The interim report made two recommendations: (1) strengthen the National Coordination Office to help it meet increasing future demands for program coordination and information functions; and (2) immediately appoint the congressionally mandated HPCCI Advisory Committee to provide broad-based, active input to the initiative. As this final report goes to press, both recommendations have yet to be acted on and thus require executive and legislative attention.

This final report, *Evolving the High Performance Computing and Communications Initiative to Support the Nation's Information Infrastructure,* purposely adopted a broad perspective so as to examine the HPCCI within the context of the evolving information infrastructure and national economic competitiveness generally. Committee deliberations consistently pointed out the important contributions that computing and communications research have made to the nation's economy, scientific research, national defense, and social fabric. That research has nourished U.S. leadership in information technology goods, services, and applications. Traditionally, the most powerful computers and the fastest networks made many of those contributions. Recently, however, the widespread availability of significant computing and communications capabilities on the nation's desktops and factory floors has also produced many benefits. The broadening and interconnection of more and more computer-based systems call attention to research needs associated with system scale as well as performance.

The Committee to Study High Performance Computing and Communications: Status of a Major Initiative is grateful for the help, encouragement, and hard work of the NRC staff working with us: Marjory Blumenthal, Jim Mallory, Susan Maurizi, and Leslie Wade. Our meetings went smoothly because of their careful preparation. This report came together because of their attention and diligence. They patiently assembled sometimes conflicting text from diverse authors and helped reconcile it with the critique of our reviewers. They searched out facts of importance to our deliberations. Their excellent staff preparation helped us focus on the substance of our task.

Many others also made valuable contributions to the committee. In addition to individuals listed in Appendix F who briefed the committee, the committee appreciates inputs from Sally Howe and Don Austin (National Coordination Office); Bob Borchers, Paul Young, Dick Kaplan, and Robert Voight (National Science Foundation); Eric Cooper (FORE Systems); Stephen Squires (Advanced Research Projects Agency); Sandy MacDonald (National Oceanic and Atmospheric Administration); Robert Bonometti (Office of Science and Technology Policy); and Al Rosenheck (former congressional staffer). It is also grateful to the anonymous reviewers who helped to sharpen and focus the report with their insightful comments. Responsibility for the report, of course, remains with the committee.

---

[1]Computer Science and Telecommunications Board (CSTB), National Research Council. 1994. *Interim Report on the Status of the High Performance Computing and Communications Initiative.* Computer Science and Telecommunications Board, Washington, D.C.

Finally, we want to acknowledge the contributions to our present task of research projects 30 years past. Of course this text was all word processed. Of course the charts were drafted on computers. Of course we used Internet communication nationwide to plan our meetings, share our thoughts, reconcile our differences, and assemble our report. We plugged our portable computers into a local network at each of our meetings, sending drafts to local laser printers. In short, we have partaken fully of the fruits of the HPCCI's precursors. We thank the visionaries of the past for our tools.

Frederick P. Brooks
Ivan E. Sutherland
Co-chairs
Committee to Study High Performance Computing and Communications:
Status of a Major Initiative

Contents

APPENDIXES

Industry, if left to itself, will naturally find its way to the most useful and profitable employment. Whence it is inferred that manufacturers, without the aid of government, will grow up as soon and as fast as the natural state of things and the interest of the community may require.

Against the solidity of this hypothesis. . . . very cogent reasons may be offered . . . [including] the strong influence of habit; the spirit of imitation; the fear of want of success in untried enterprises; the intrinsic difficulties incident to first essays towards [competition with established foreign players]: the bounties, premiums, and other artificial encouragements with which foreign nations second the exertions of their own citizens. . . . To produce the desirable changes as early as may be expedient may therefore require the incitement and patronage of government.

—Alexander Hamilton, 1791, *Report on Manufactures*

Executive Summary

Information technology drives many of today's innovations and offers still greater potential for further innovation in the next decade. It is also the basis for a domestic industry of about $500 billion,[1] an industry that is critical to our nation's international competitiveness. Our domestic information technology industry is thriving now, based to a large extent on an extraordinary 50-year track record of public research funded by the federal government, creating the ideas and people that have let industry flourish. This record shows that for a dozen major innovations, 10 to 15 years have passed between research and commercial application (see Figure ES.1). Despite many efforts, commercialization has seldom been achieved more quickly.

Publicly funded research in information technology will continue to create important new technologies and industries, some of them unimagined today, and the process will continue to take 10 to 15 years. Without such research there will still be innovation, but the quantity and range of new ideas for U.S. industry to draw from will be greatly diminished. Public research, which creates new opportunities for private industry to use, should not be confused with industrial policy, which chooses firms or industries to support. Industry, with its focus mostly on the near term, cannot take the place of government in supporting the research that will lead to the next decade's advances.

The High Performance Computing and Communications Initiative (HPCCI) is the main vehicle for public research in information technology today and the subject of this report. By the early 1980s, several federal agencies had developed independent programs to advance many of the objectives of what was to become the HPCCI. The program received added impetus and more formal status when Congress passed the High Performance Computing Act of 1991 (Public Law 102-194) authorizing a 5-year program in high-performance computing and communications. The initiative began with a focus on high-speed parallel computing and networking and is now evolving to meet the needs of the nation for widespread use on a large scale as well as for high speed in computation and communications. To advance the nation's information infrastructure there is much that needs to be discovered or invented, because a useful "information highway" is much more than wires to every house.

As a prelude to examining the current status of the HPCCI, this report first describes the rationale for the initiative as an engine of U.S. leadership in information technology and outlines the contributions of ongoing publicly funded research to past and current progress in developing computing and communications technologies (Chapter 1). It then describes and evaluates the HPCCI's goals, accomplishments, management, and planning (Chapter 2). Finally, it makes recommendations aimed at ensuring continuing U.S. leadership in information technology through wise evolution and use of the HPCCI as an important lever (Chapter 3). Appendixes A through F of the report provide additional details on and documentation for points made in the main text.

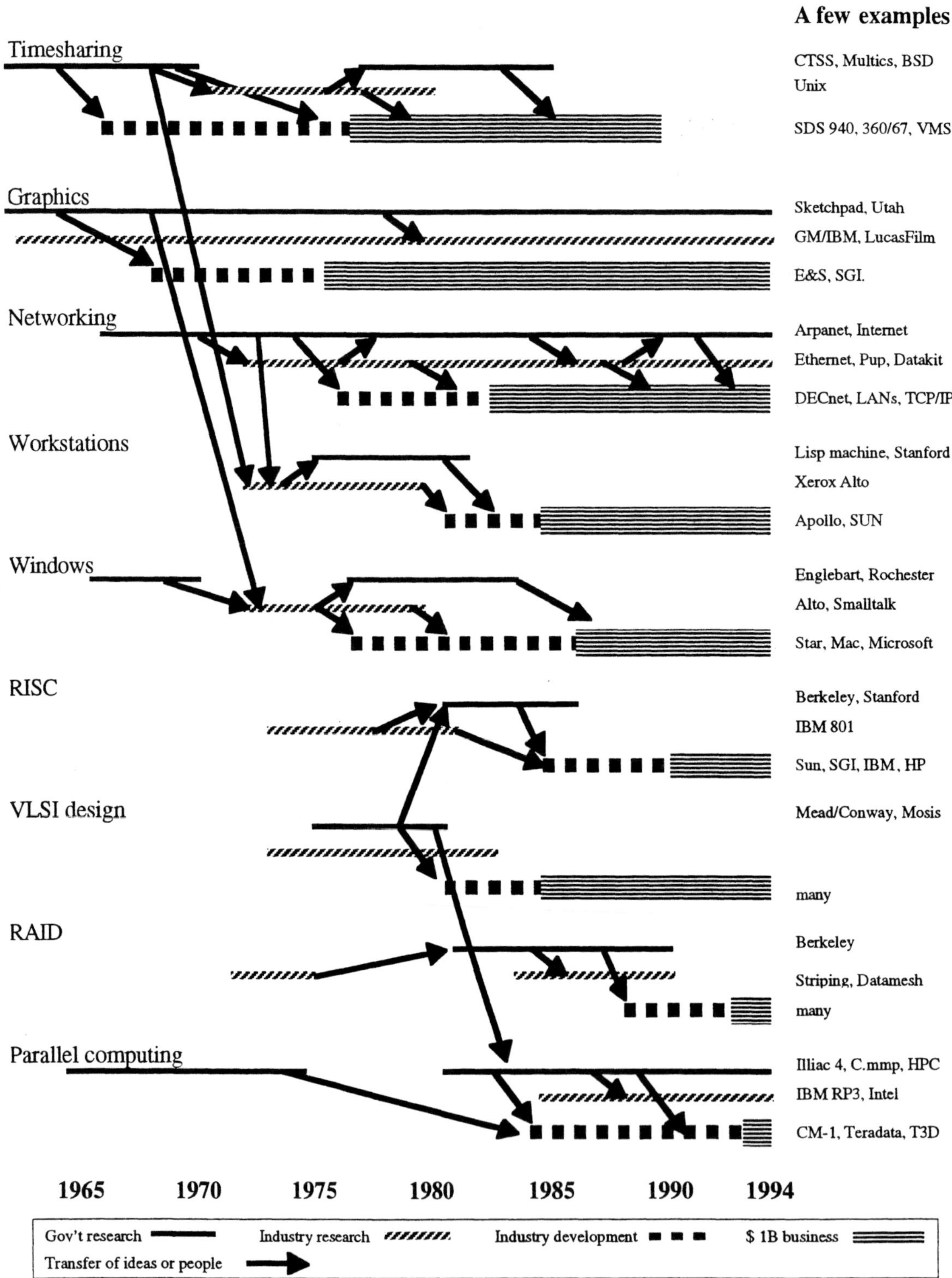

FIGURE ES.1 Government-sponsored computing research and development stimulates creation of innovative ideas and industries. Dates apply to horizontal bars, but not to arrows showing transfer of ideas and people.

INFORMATION TECHNOLOGY—FUNDAMENTAL FOR SOCIETY AND THE ECONOMY NOW AND TOMORROW

Computers, the devices that process information, affect our lives both directly and indirectly. Today, more than 70 million microcomputers are installed in the United States, and between one-fifth and one-third of U.S. households have one.[2] Entertainment, education, communications, medicine, government, and finance are using computers in more ways to enhance our lives directly through the provision of such services as distributed learning and remote banking. Computers are also used to make essential products and activities cheaper and better: airplanes, molded plastics, automobiles, medical imaging, and oil exploration are only a few of many examples. A broader benefit is the $500 billion industry's creation of jobs, taxes, profits, and exports.

Clearly, the uses and applications of information technology will continue to grow. In fact, the information revolution has only just begun. Computers will become increasingly valuable to industries and to citizens as their power is tapped to recognize and simulate speech, generate realistic images, provide accurate models of the physical world, build huge automated libraries, control robots, and help with a myriad of other tasks. To do these things well will require both computing and communications systems many times more powerful than we have today. Ongoing advances in knowledge will constitute the foundation for building the systems and developing the applications that will continue to advance our quality of life and ensure strong U.S. leadership in information technology. Strong leadership in information technology in turn supports other sectors including industry, health, education, and defense by serving their needs for equipment, software, and know-how.

The Basis for Continuing Strength— A Successful Government-Industry Partnership

Federal investment in information technology research has played a key role in the U.S. capability to maintain its international lead in information technology. Starting in World War II publicly funded research has helped to stock the nation's storehouse of trained people and innovative ideas. But our lead is fragile. Leadership can shift in a few product generations, and because a generation in the computing and communications industry is at most 2 years, our lead could disappear in less than a decade.

Since the early 1960s the U.S. government has invested broadly in computing research, creating new ideas and trained people. The result has been the development of important new technologies for time-sharing, networking, computer graphics, human-machine interfaces, and parallel computing, as well as major contributions to the design of very large scale integrated circuits, fast computers and disk systems, and workstations (see Figure ES.1; see also Chapter 1, Box 1.2 for details). Each of these is now a multibillion-dollar business. From these successes we can learn some important lessons:

- *Research has kept paying off over a long period.*

- *The payoff from research takes time.* As Figure ES.1 shows, at least 10 years, more often 15, elapse between initial research on a major new idea and commercial success. This is still true in spite of today's shorter product cycles.

- *Unexpected results are often the most important.* Electronic mail and the "windows" interface are only two examples; Box 1.2 in Chapter 1 outlines more.

• *Research stimulates communication and interaction.* Ideas flow back and forth between research programs and development efforts and between academia and industry.

• *Research trains people,* who start companies or form a pool of trained personnel that existing companies can draw on to enter new markets quickly.

• *Doing research involves taking risks.* Not all public research programs have succeeded or led to clear outcomes even after many years. But the record of accomplishments suggests that government investment in computing and communications research has been very productive.

Government Support of Research Is Crucial

The information technology industry improves its products faster than most others: for the last 40 years a dollar has bought hardware with twice as much computation, storage, and communication every 18 to 24 months, offering a 100-fold gain every decade (Patterson and Hennessy, 1994, p. 21). This rate will continue at least for the next decade (see Chapter 1, Figure 1.1). Better hardware in turn makes it feasible to create software for new applications: electronic and mechanical design, climate mapping, digital libraries, desktop publishing, video editing, and telemedicine are just a few examples. Such applications are often brought to market by new companies such as Microsoft and Sun Microsystems, both of which produce revenues of more than $4 billion per year (Computer Select, 1994) and neither of which existed 15 years ago.

The information technology industry is characterized by great importance to the economy and society, rapid and continuing change, a 10- to 15-year cycle from major idea to commercial success, and successive waves of new companies. In this environment a broad program of publicly funded research is essential for two reasons:

• First, industrial efforts cannot replace government investment in basic computing and communications research. Few companies will invest for a payoff that is 10 years away, and even a company that does make a discovery may postpone using it. The vitality of the information technology industry depends heavily on new companies, but new companies cannot easily afford to do research; furthermore, industry in general is doing less research now than in the recent past (Geppert, 1994; Corcoran, 1994). But because today's sales are based on yesterday's research, investment in innovation must go forward so that the nation's information industry can continue to thrive.

• Second, it is hard to predict which new ideas and approaches will succeed. The exact course of exploratory research cannot be planned in advance, and its progress cannot be measured precisely in the short term. The purpose of publicly funded research is to advance knowledge and create new opportunities that industry can exploit in the medium and long term, not to determine how the market should develop.

THE HIGH PERFORMANCE COMPUTING AND COMMUNICATIONS INITIATIVE

Goals and Emphases

The HPCCI is the current manifestation of the continuing government research program in information technology, an investment that has been ongoing for more than 50 years. Although it emphasizes research in high-performance computing and communications, the HPCCI now has in its budget nearly all of the federal funding for computing research of any kind. The wisdom of this arrangement is doubtful.

The HPCCI was initiated to serve several broad goals (NCO, 1993):

- Extend U.S. leadership in high-performance computing and networking;
- Disseminate new technologies to serve the economy, national security, education, health care, and the environment; and
- Spur gains in U.S. productivity and industrial competitiveness.

The original plans to achieve these goals called for creating dramatically faster computers and networks, stretching their limits with Grand Challenge problems in scientific computing, setting up supercomputer centers with the machines and experts needed to attack these challenges, and training people to build and exploit the new technology. More recently the focus has been shifting toward broader uses of computing and communications.

High Performance

"High performance"—which involves bringing more powerful computing and communications technology to bear on a problem—has enabled advances on several fronts. High-performance systems, for example, deliver answers sooner for complex problems that need large amounts of computing. Timely and accurate forecasting of weather, mapping of oil reservoirs, and imaging of tumors are among the benefits encompassed by the goals listed above. But "high performance," which is broader than supercomputing, is a moving target because of the steady and rapid gains in the performance/cost ratio. Yesterday's supercomputer is today's personal computer; today's leading-edge communications technology will be among tomorrow's mainstream capabilities.

Information technology evolves as new and valuable applications are found for hardware that gets steadily more powerful and cheaper. To benefit, users need affordable hardware, but they also need the software that implements the new applications. Yet learning how to build software takes many years of experimentation. If this process starts only when the hardware has already become cheap, the benefits to users will be delayed by years. Research needs to treat today's expensive equipment as a time machine, learning how it will be used when it is cheap and widely available, as it surely will be tomorrow. Knowing how to use computers for new tasks sooner can help many industries to become more competitive.

To date, the HPCCI's focus has been mainly on speed, but speed is not the only measure of high performance. Both speed, measured today in billions of operations per second or billions of bits per second, and scale, measured by the number of millions of users served, are important research issues. However, for the nation's information infrastructure, scale now seems more difficult to achieve. Information technology can be thought of as a tent, with the height of the center pole as speed and the breadth of the base as scale. Widening the tent to allow more work on scale without decreasing the work on speed requires more cloth; with the same resources, widening the tent would sacrifice research on speed for research on scale. This report recommends ways to reallocate funds within the HPCCI so as to accommodate greater emphasis on scale.

Accomplishments to Date

The HPCCI has focused mainly on parallel computing, networking, and development of human resources. Building on progress in research begun before the HPCCI, work and accomplishments to date reveal two key trends: better computing and computational infrastructure and increasing researcher-developer-user synergy.

Despite the difficulty of measuring impact at this early stage, it is the committee's judgment that the HPCCI has been generally successful so far. That assessment is necessarily qualitative and experiential now. Because the HPCCI is only 3 years old, results that can be measured in dollars should not be expected before the next decade.

The HPCCI has contributed substantially to the development, deployment, and understanding of computing and communications facilities and capabilities as infrastructure. It has helped transform understanding of how to share resources and information, generating proofs of concept and understanding that are of value not only to the scientific research community but also to the economy and society at large.

In parallel computing the fundamental challenge is not building the machines, but learning how to program them. Pioneering users and their software developers must be motivated by machines that are good enough to reward success with significant speedups.[3] For this reason, a great deal of money and effort have had to be spent to obtain parallel machines with the potential to run much faster than existing supercomputers. From the base built by the HPCCI, much has been learned about parallel computing.

The HPCCI has fostered productive interactions among the researchers and developers involved in creating high-performance computing and communications technology and researchers who use the technology. Building on the varying perspectives of the three groups, complex problems are being solved in unique ways. In particular, the HPCCI has funded cross-disciplinary teams associated with the Grand Challenge projects to solve complex computational problems and produce essential new software for the new parallel systems.

More specifically, the HPCCI has:

- Increased the nation's stock of expertise by educating new students and attracting new researchers;

- Made parallel computing widely accepted as the practical route to achieving high-performance computing;

- Demonstrated the feasibility of and initiated deployment of parallel databases;

- Driven progress on Grand Challenge problems in disciplines such as cosmology, molecular biology, chemistry, and materials science. Parallel computation has enhanced the ability to attack problems of great complexity in science and engineering;

- Developed new modes of analyzing and visualizing complex data sets in the earth sciences, medicine, molecular biology, and engineering, including creating virtual reality technologies. Many supercomputer graphic techniques of the 1980s are now available on desktop graphics workstations;

• Through the gigabit network testbeds associated with the National Research and Education Network component, demonstrated the intimate link between computing and communications systems;

• Built advanced networks that are the backbone of the Internet and the prototypes for its further evolution into the basis for a broader information infrastructure;

• Deployed a high-speed backbone that has kept up with the yearly doubling of the size of the Internet, and organized the impending transition of this backbone away from government funding; and

• Created the Mosaic browser for the World Wide Web, the first new major application in many years that promises to greatly increase access to the resources available on the Internet. This was an entirely unexpected result.

Evolution

A large-scale, integrated information infrastructure designed to serve the entire nation is becoming a high priority for government and industry as well as a source of challenges for research. Complex systems with millions of users pose many problems: performance, management, security, interoperability, compatible evolution of components, mobility, and reliability are only a few. Today's technology can solve these problems for systems with a few thousand users at most; to do so for millions or hundreds of millions of users is far beyond the current state of the art.[4] Providing users with high-bandwidth connections is itself a major problem, but it is only the beginning. There is a wide gap between enabling a connection and providing a rich array of useful and dependable services.

Because the HPCCI has become the rubric under which virtually all of the nation's research in information technology is conducted, it is not surprising that its focus has been changing in response to past successes, new opportunities, and evolving societal needs. The recently added Information Infrastructure Technology and Applications (IITA) program, broadly construed, addresses many of the problems just mentioned; it is already the largest component of the HPCCI,[5] and its continued evolution should be encouraged.

But with the policy focus—in the government, the press, and in most of the agencies—centered on information infrastructure,[6] high-performance computing seems to have been downplayed. The committee emphasizes the importance of retaining the HPCCI's momentum at just the time when its potential to support improvement in the nation's information infrastructure is most needed.

Organization

Several federal agencies participate in the HPCCI, most notably the National Science Foundation (NSF), the Advanced Research Projects Agency (ARPA), the National Aeronautics and Space Administration (NASA), and the Department of Energy (DOE) (see Appendix A for a full list). Because of its successes the HPCCI has become a model for multiagency collaboration and for the "virtual agency" concept advanced through the *National Performance Review* (Gore, 1993). Each participating agency retains responsibility for its own part of the program, but the agencies work together in joint funding of projects, such as the federal portions of the Internet; joint reviews of grants and contracts, such as the NSF-ARPA-NASA digital library initiative; joint testbeds; and consortia, such as the consortium for Advanced Modeling of Regional Air Quality that joins six federal agencies with several state and local governments.

The HPCCI supports a diverse set of contractors at universities, companies, and national laboratories throughout the country. It provides project funding in varying amounts through contracts, grants, and cooperative agreements awarded according to diverse methods. This diversity is healthy because it allows many views to compete, resulting in a broad research program that ensures a continuing flow of advances in information technology.

Some have argued for a more centrally managed program, with thorough planning, precise milestones, and presumably no wasted effort. Tighter management would cost more in bureaucracy and turf wars, but the essential question is whether it would produce better or worse results for the money spent. The committee believes that because of the long time scale of research, diversity is essential for success. No one person or organization is either smart or lucky enough to plan the best program, no single approach is best, and success often comes in unanticipated ways. Because it is a national research program and because of the many different but interdependent underlying technologies, the HPCCI is necessarily and properly far more diverse than a focused effort such as the Apollo moon landing program or a commercial product development program.

In contrast to central management, coordination enhances the benefits of diversity by helping to prevent unintended duplication, redundancy, and missed opportunities. The HPCCI's National Coordination Office (NCO) serves this purpose, aiding interagency cooperation and acting as liaison for the initiative to the Congress, other levels of government, universities, industry, and the public. Its efforts are reflected in its impressive FY 1994 and FY 1995 "Blue Books" describing the program's activities and spending.[7] Strengthening the NCO and appointing an advisory committee, as recommended in the committee's interim report (CSTB, 1994c), would facilitate regular infusions of ideas and advice from industry and academia and enable better communication of the HPCCI's goals and accomplishments to its many constituents. This committee should consist of a group of recognized experts that is balanced between academia and industry and balanced with respect to application areas and the core technologies underlying the HPCCI.

Budget

Because it grew from earlier programs, a significant portion of the HPCCI budget is not new money. The budget grew from a base of $490 million in preexisting funding in FY 1992 to the $1.1 billion requested for FY 1995.[8] Each year agencies have added to the base by moving budgets for existing programs into the HPCCI and by reprogramming existing funds to support the HPCCI. Congress has also added funding each year to start new activities or expand old ones.

The result is that much of the $1.1 billion requested for FY 1995 is money that was already being spent on computing and communications in FY 1992. The request has three elements: (1) funds for activities that predate the HPCCI and were in the FY 1992 base budget, (2) funds for activities that have since been designated as part of the HPCCI, and (3) new funds for new activities or for growth. Although dissecting the budget in this way would shed light on the program, the committee was unable to do so because each participating agency treats the numbers differently.

It appears that the FY 1995 request breaks down roughly as one-third for applications, one-third to advance the essential underlying computing and communications technologies, one-quarter for computing and communications infrastructure, and small amounts for education and electronics (see Appendix C).

THE FUTURE OF THE HPCCI: RECOMMENDATIONS

The committee believes that strong public support for a broadly based research program in information technology is vital to maintaining U.S. leadership in information technology. Incorporating this view of the importance and success of the government's investment in research, the 13 recommendations that follow address five areas: general research program, high-performance computing, networking and information infrastructure, the supercomputer centers and the Grand Challenge projects, and program coordination and management. Within each area the recommendations are presented in priority order.

General Recommendations

1. Continue to support research in information technology. Ensure that the major funding agencies, especially the National Science Foundation and the Advanced Research Projects Agency, have strong programs for computing and communications research that are independent of any special initiatives.

The government investment in computing research has yielded significant returns. Ongoing investment, *at least as high as the current dollar level*, is critical both to U.S. leadership and to ongoing innovation in information technology. Today the HPCCI supports nearly all of this research, an arrangement that is both misleading and dangerous: misleading because much important computing research addresses areas other than high performance (even though it may legitimately fit under the new IITA component of the HPCCI), and dangerous because reduced funding for the HPCCI could cripple all of computing research. The "war on cancer" did not support all of biomedical research, and neither should the HPCCI or any future initiative on national infrastructure subsume all of computing research.

2. Continue the HPCCI, maintaining today's increased emphasis on the research challenges posed by the nation's evolving information infrastructure. The new Information Infrastructure Technology and Applications program of the HPCCI focuses on information infrastructure topics, which are also addressed in the initiative's other four components. The committee supports this continued evolution, which will lead to tangible returns on existing and future investments in basic hardware, networking, and software technologies.

High-Performance Computing

3. Continue funding a strong experimental research program in software and algorithms for parallel computing machines. Today a crucial obstacle to widespread use of parallel computing is the lack of advanced software and algorithms. Emphasis should be given to research on developing and building usable applications-oriented software systems for parallel computers. **Avoid funding the transfer ("porting") of existing commercial applications to new parallel computing machines unless there is a specific research need.**

4. Stop direct HPCCI funding for development of commercial hardware by computer vendors and for "industrial stimulus" purchases of hardware. Maintain HPCCI support for precompetitive research in computer architecture; this work should be done in universities or in university-industry collaborations and should be driven by the needs of system and application software. HPCCI funding for stimulus purchase of large-scale machines has been reduced, as has the funding of hardware development by vendors. The committee supports these changes, which should continue except when a mission need demands the development of nonstandard hardware.

Public research is best done in universities. Not only are academic organizations free to think about longer-term issues, but they also stimulate technology transfer through publication and placement of graduates. The national experience supports Vannevar Bush's basic tenet: publicly funded research carried out in universities produces a diversity of excellent ideas, trained people, research results, and technologies that can be commercially exploited (OSRD and Bush, 1945).

5. Treat development of a teraflop computer as a research direction rather than a destination. The goal of developing teraflop capability has served a valuable purpose in stimulating work on large-scale parallelism, but further investment in raw scalability is inappropriate except as a focus for precompetitive, academic research. Industrial development of parallel computers will balance the low cost of individual, mass-produced computing devices against the higher cost of communicating between them in a variety of interesting ways. In the near future a teraflop parallel machine will be built when some agencies' mission requirements correspond to a sufficiently economical commercial offering. Continued progress will surely lead to machines even larger than a teraflop.

Networking and Information Infrastructure

New ideas are needed to meet the new challenges underlying development of the nation's information infrastructure. The HPCCI can contribute most by focusing on the underlying research issues. This shift has already begun, and it should continue.

This evolution of the research agenda, which would support improvement of the nation's information infrastructure, is partly under way: in the *FY 1995 Implementation Plan* (NCO, 1994, p. 15), over one-quarter of the NSF and ARPA HPCCI funding is focused on the IITA component, and activities in other components have also evolved consistent with these concerns. The committee supports this increased emphasis.

6. Increase the HPCCI focus on communications and networking research, especially on the challenges inherent in scale and physical distribution. An integrated information infrastructure that fully serves the nation's needs cannot spring full-grown from what we already know. Much research is needed on difficult problems related to size, evolution, introduction of new systems, reliability, and interoperability. Much more is involved than simply deploying large numbers of boxes and wires. For example, both hardware and software systems must work efficiently to handle scheduling; bandwidth optimization for transmission of a range of data formats, including real-time audio and video data; protocol and format conversion; security; and many other requirements.

7. Develop a research program to address the research challenges underlying our ability to build very large, reliable, high-performance, distributed information systems based on the existing HPCCI foundation. Although a comprehensive vision of the research needed for advancing the nation's information infrastructure has not yet been developed, three key areas for research are scalability, physical distribution, and interoperative applications.

8. Ensure that research programs focusing on the National Challenges contribute to the development of information infrastructure technologies as well as to the development of new applications and paradigms. This dual emphasis contrasts with the narrower focus on scientific results that has driven work on the Grand Challenges.

Supercomputer Centers and Grand Challenge Program

The NSF supercomputer centers have played a major role in establishing parallel computing as a full partner with the prior paradigms of scalar and vector computing by providing access to state-of-the-art computing facilities. NSF should continue to take a broad view of the centers' mission of providing access to high-performance computing and communications resources, including participating in research needed to improve software for parallel machines and to advance the nation's information infrastructure.

The committee recognizes that advanced computation is an important tool for scientists and and engineers and that support for adequate computer access must be a part of the NSF research program in all disciplines. The committee did not consider the appropriate overall funding level for the centers. However, the committee believes that NSF should move to a model similar to that used by NASA and DOE for funding general access to computing. The committee prefers NASA's and DOE's approach to funding supercomputer centers, where HPCCI funds are used only to support the exploration and use of new computing architectures, while non-HPCCI funds are used to support general access.

9. The mission of the National Science Foundation supercomputer centers remains important, but the NSF should continue to evaluate new directions, alternative funding mechanisms, new administrative structures, and the overall program level of the centers. NSF could continue funding of the centers at the current level or alter that level, but it should continue using HPCCI funds to support applications that contribute to the evolution of the underlying computing and communications technologies, while support for general access by application scientists to maturing architectures should come increasingly from non-HPCCI funds.

10. The Grand Challenge program is an innovative approach to creating interdisciplinary and multi-institutional scientific research teams; however, continued use of HPCCI funds is appropriate only when the research contributes significantly to the development of new high-performance computing and communications hardware or software. Grand Challenge projects funded under the HPCCI should be evaluated on the basis of their contributions both to high-performance computing and communications technologies and to the application area. Completion of the Grand Challenge projects will provide valuable insights and demonstrate the capabilities of new high-performance architectures in some important applications. It will also foster better collaboration between computer scientists and computational scientists. The committee notes that a large share of HPCCI funding for the Grand Challenges currently comes from the scientific disciplines involved. However, the overall funding seems to come entirely from HPCCI-labeled funds. For the same reasons outlined in Recommendation 9, the committee sees this commingled support as unhealthy in the long run and urges a transition to greater reliance on scientific disciplinary funding using non-HPCCI funds.

Coordination and Program Management

11. Strengthen the HPCCI National Coordination Office while retaining the cooperative structure of the HPCCI and increasing the opportunity for external input. Immediately appoint the congressionally mandated advisory committee intended to provide broad-based, active input to the HPCCI, or provide an effective alternative. Appoint an individual to be a full-time coordinator, program spokesperson, and advocate for the HPCCI.

In making this recommendation, the committee strongly endorses the role of the current NCO as supporting the mission agencies rather than directing them. The committee believes it vital that the separate agencies retain direction of their HPCCI funds. The value of interagency cooperation outweighs any benefits that might be gained through more centralized management.

Diverse management systems for research should be welcomed, and micromanagement should be avoided. In the past, choosing good program officers and giving them freedom to operate independently have yielded good value, and the committee believes it will continue to do so.

Furthermore, independence will encourage diversity in the research program, thus increasing opportunities for unexpected discoveries, encouraging a broader attack on problems, and ensuring fewer missed opportunities.

12. Place projects in the HPCCI only if they match well to its objectives. Federal research funding agencies should promptly document the extent to which HPCCI funding is supporting important long-term research areas whose future funding should be independent of the future of the HPCCI.

A number of preexisting agency programs have entered the HPCCI, with two effects: the HPCCI's budget appears to grow faster than the real growth of investment in high-performance computing and communications research, and important programs such as basic research in computing within NSF and ARPA may be in jeopardy should the HPCCI end.

13. Base mission agency computer procurements on mission needs only, and encourage making equipment procurement decisions at the lowest practical management level. This recommendation applies equally to government agencies and to government contractors. It has generally been best for an agency to specify the results it wants and to leave the choice of specific equipment to the contractor or local laboratory management.

NOTES

1. See U.S. DOC (1994); the Department of Commerce utilizes data from the U.S. Bureau of the Census series, the *Annual Survey of Manufactures*. It places the value of shipments for the information technology industry at $421 billion for 1993. This number omits revenue from equipment rentals, fees for after-sale service, and mark-ups in the product distribution channel. It also excludes office equipment in total. It includes computers, storage devices, terminals and peripherals; packaged software; computer program manufacturing, data processing, information services, facilities management, and other services; and telecommunications equipment and services.

See also CBEMA (1994); CBEMA values the worldwide 1993 revenue of the U.S. information technology industry at $602 billion. In addition to including office equipment, it shows larger revenues for information technology hardware and telecommunications equipment than does the Department of Commerce.

2. Microcomputers (personal computers) are defined as computers with a list price of $1,000 to $14,999; see CBEMA (1994), pp. 60-61. Forrester Research Inc. (1994, pp. 2-3) estimates the share of households with PCs at about 20 percent, based on its survey of households and Bureau of Census data. Forrester's model accounts for retirements of older PCs and for households with multiple PCs. This is a lower estimate than the Software Publishing Association's widely cited 30 percent share. By definition, the microcomputer statistics exclude small computers and other general-purpose and specialized devices that also make use of microprocessors and would be counted in a more comprehensive measurement of information technology.

3. Earlier experience with three isolated computers, "Illiac 4" (built at the University of Illinois) and "C.mmp" and "Cm*" (both built at Carnegie Mellon University), bears out this point.

4. Of course, systems specialized for a single application or for homogenous technology, such as telephony, serve millions of users, but what is now envisioned is more complex and heterogenous, involving integration of multiple services and systems.

5. The other four programs of the HPCCI are Advanced Software Technology and Algorithms, Basic Research and Human Resources, High-Performance Computing Systems, and the National Research and Education Network.

6. Notably, references to the computing portion of the HPCCI have been overshadowed recently by the ubiquity of speeches and documents devoted to the notion of a national information infrastructure (NII). The NII has also been featured in the titles of the 1994 and 1995 Blue Books.

7. Each year beginning in 1991 the director of the Office of Science and Technology Policy submits a report on the HPCCI to accompany the president's budget. The FY 1992, FY 1993, and FY 1994 books were produced by the now-defunct Federal Coordinating Council for Science, Engineering, and Technology; the FY 1995 report was produced by the NCO (acting for the Committee on Information and Communications). The report describes prior accomplishments and the future funding and activities for the coming fiscal year. These reports have collectively become known as "Blue Books" after the color of their cover.

8. NCO (1994), p. 15. Note that figures represent the President's requested budget authority for FY 1995. Actual appropriated levels were not available at press time. Because the HPCCI is synthesized as a cross-cutting multiagency initiative, there is no separate and identifiable "HPCCI appropriation."

1
U.S. Leadership in Information Technology

Information technology is central to our economy and society. The United States has held a commanding lead in this arena, a lead that we must maintain. Meeting the challenges posed by rapid, worldwide change will continue to require our best efforts to advance the state of the art in computing and communications technology. Now, as in the past, our ability to lead requires an ongoing strong program of long-term research. The federal government has supported such research for 50 years with great success.

Today, the High Performance Computing and Communications Initiative (HPCCI) is the multiagency cooperative effort under which most of this research is funded. For this reason, any discussion of the HPCCI must be grounded in an understanding of the role and nature of information technology, the information industry, and the nation's research program in computing. These issues are the subject of this first chapter of the report.

INFORMATION TECHNOLOGY IS CENTRAL TO OUR SOCIETY

Computers affect our lives enormously. We use them directly for everyday tasks such as making an airline reservation, getting money from an automated teller machine, or writing a report on a word processor. We also enjoy many products and services that would not be possible without digital computing and communications.

The direct use of computing is growing rapidly. Personal computers are already pervasive in our economy and society: in the United States over 70 million are installed, and between one-fifth and one-third of U.S. households have a computer.[1] The increasing popularity of personal computing is but the tip of the iceberg; education, communication, medicine, government, manufacturing, transportation, science, engineering, finance, and entertainment all increasingly use digital computing and communications to enhance our lives directly by offering improved goods and services.

Indirectly, computing and communications are used to make many products cheaper and better. Without computers connected by communication networks, designing the newest U.S. jetliner, the Boeing 777, within acceptable cost and time constraints would have been impossible. Advanced hardware and advanced software working together substituted computer models for expensive and time-consuming physical modeling. The design of complex plastic molded parts, now routinely used for many products, depends on computer simulation of plastic flow and computer control of die making. Automobile engines rely on embedded computers for fuel economy and emission control, and doctors use computer-assisted tomography (CAT) scanners to see inside the body. Computers help us understand and tap Earth's resources: our oil is found by computer analysis of geologic data. Interconnected computer systems underlie our entire financial system, enabling electronic funds transfer and services such as home banking. Digital communication extends to a large and rapidly increasing number of businesses, educational institutions, government agencies, and homes.

Originally devices for computation and business data processing, computers now are tools for information access and processing in the broadest sense. As such, they have become fundamental to the operation of our society, and computing and communications have come to be labeled widely as "information processing."

Remarkably, given its already enormous direct and indirect impact, information technology is being deployed in our society more rapidly now than at any time in the past.[2] If this momentum is sustained, then digital technology and digital information—the digital information revolution—will offer a huge range of new applications, create markets for a wide variety of new products and services, and yield a broad spectrum of benefits to all Americans.

INFORMATION TECHNOLOGY ADVANCES RAPIDLY

The information industry improves its products with amazing speed. For several decades—powered by federal and industrial research and development (R&D) investments in computer science, computer engineering, electrical engineering, and semiconductor physics—each dollar spent on computation, storage, and communication has bought twice the performance every 18 to 24 months. Over the course of each decade, this sustained rate of progress results in a 100-fold improvement, as Figure 1.1 shows for processor speed and disk storage capacity. With continued investment, we can sustain this rate of progress for at least the next decade. Such rapid improvement is possible because of the nature of information and of the technologies required to process it: integrated circuits, storage devices, and communications systems (Box 1.1). Significant improvements in hardware performance in turn make it feasible to create the software required for computers to do new things—electronic and mechanical design, desktop publishing, video editing, modeling of financial markets, creation of digital libraries, and the practice of telemedicine, for example.

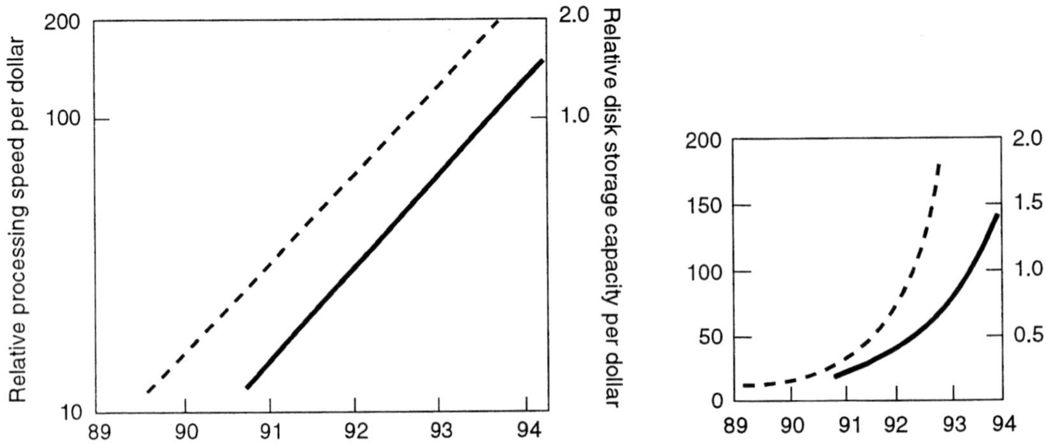

FIGURE 1.1 Increase in performance per dollar of processor speed and disk storage from 1989 to 1994, shown on a semilog scale. (The right-hand graph uses a linear scale to emphasize the compound effect of successive doublings.)

BOX 1.1 What Drives the Progress in Information Technology?

• *Integrated circuits improve rapidly.* Computers are made from integrated circuits, each component of which gets half as high and half as wide every 5 years, with the result that the same area can hold four times as many components at the same cost. Also, each component runs twice as fast, and the circuit chips get bigger. The physical limits to this progress are still far off.

• *New designs take advantage of advances in integrated circuits.* Today's microprocessors and memories are made from very large scale integrated (VLSI) circuits. Although modern VLSI microprocessors and memories may have 10 million components, they are actually designed in no more time than the integrated circuits of a decade ago that had only 100,000 components. Advances in designs and design tools—in our ability to master complexity—have been, and will continue to be, essential to taking advantage of advances in integrated circuit technology.

• *It is cheap to make more devices, and the same integrated circuit foundries can make many different devices.* The marginal cost of building more computers is small, because the cost of raw materials is low and the components are mass-produced. Further, although an integrated circuit foundry may be expensive to build, it can make many different products, just as a printing press can print many different books. Because the same process is used over and over again, improvements in this process have enormous effects on product cost and quality.

• *New designs can quickly become products.* A new digital system is usually built in an existing foundry that operates directly from a digital description of the design. Investing in prototypes is not necessary, because it is possible to simulate a product accurately and automatically from the design.

• *Dramatic system advances enable dramatic application advances.* The fact that computing power per dollar doubles every 18 months means that capabilities can migrate from the high end to the consumer rapidly and predictably. It is R&D investment at the high end that creates these capabilities. Today's desktop workstation was the supercomputer of a mere decade ago. Today's solutions to the problems of large-scale parallelism will enable us to solve tomorrow's mass-market problems of on-chip parallelism.

Rapid progress has produced successive waves of new companies in diverse areas related to information technology and its applications: integrated circuits, computer hardware, computer software, communications, embedded systems, robotics, video on demand, and others. Many of today's major hardware and software firms, including Sun Microsystems and Microsoft, both with revenues of more than $4 billion per year (Computer Select, 1994), did not exist 15 years ago, and none except IBM and Unisys were in the information business 40 years ago. Many of these new companies have drawn on ideas and people from federally funded research projects.

RETAINING LEADERSHIP IN INFORMATION TECHNOLOGY IS VITAL TO THE NATION

The U.S. lead in information technology has brought benefits that are clearly valuable to the nation:

• *The jobs and profits generated by the industry itself.* The information technology industry is big: Revenues attributable to hardware and software sales plus associated services were on the order of $500 billion in 1993.[3] Due to the limitations of what is actually counted in any given estimate, this figure may be conservative. The jobs and profits that the information technology industry complex delivers are worth careful preservation.

• *The advantages that other sectors gain from early access to the best information technology, ahead of our international competitors.* Learning how to use computers for new tasks sooner allows firms to capture new market segments and compete more efficiently in old ones. U.S. competitiveness in engineering, manufacturing, transportation, financial services, and a host of other areas depends on U.S. competitiveness in information technology (CSTB, 1994b, 1995).

• *The benefits that our citizens gain from information technology in their daily lives.* Benefits are evident in education, medicine, finance, communication, entertainment, information services, and other areas. The lives of Americans are improved by 24-hour banking, improved fuel economy in automobiles, noninvasive medical diagnosis, and hundreds of uses of computers for generating film sequences and as the basis for computerized games. The reach and impact of such applications are increasing rapidly.

Our lead in information technology is fragile, and it will slip away if we fail to adapt. Leadership has often shifted in a few product generations, and a generation in the information industry can be less than 2 years. As a nation we must continue to foster the flow of fresh ideas and trained minds that have enabled the U.S. information technology enterprise as a whole to remain strong despite the fate of individual companies. International competition is fierce, and it is likely to increase. In the mid-1980s Japan and Europe recognized the strategic importance of information technology and began investing massively in the Fifth Generation and Esprit efforts, respectively. Although these efforts did not yield new technologies to rival our own, their very significant investments in research and technology infrastructure are laying the foundation for future challenges.[4]

Today, through the efforts of government, academia, and industry, our nation retains its lead and continues to enjoy the benefits associated with it. Although many factors contributed, the committee believes that federal investment in the advancement of information technology has played a key role.

Indeed, for nearly 50 years federal investment has helped to train the people and stimulate the ideas that have made today's computers and many of their applications possible. Federal support early in the life cycle of many ideas has advanced them from novelties to convincing demonstrations that attract private investment to products and services that ultimately add to the quality of U.S. life.

THE FEDERAL INVESTMENT IN COMPUTING RESEARCH HAS PAID RICH DIVIDENDS

In the 1940s and 1950s, much of the federal investment in computing research was for defense (Flamm, 1988). Technical needs such as fire control and intelligence needs such as cryptography and mission planning required great computing power.

Since the early 1960s the federal government has invested more broadly in computing research, and these investments have profoundly affected how computers are made and used, contributed to the development of innovative ideas and training of key people, and led to the kinds of advances sampled in Table 1.1. Figure 1.2 shows the corresponding timelines for progress from research topics commercially successful applications. Notable among the government efforts stimulating many of these advances have been the Advanced Research Projects Agency's (ARPA's)

VLSI program, an initiative of the past decade (Box 1.2), and federal sponsorship of research in laying the groundwork for the now-ubiquitous field of computer graphics (Box 1.3) and for sophisticated database systems (Box 1.4).

TABLE 1.1 Some Successes of Government Funding of Computing and Communications Research

Topic	Goal	Unanticipated Results	Today
Timesharing	Let many people use a computer, each as if it were his or her own, sharing the cost.	Because many people kept their work in one computer, they could easily share information. Reduced cost increased the diversity of users and applications.	Even personal computers are timeshared among multiple applications. Information sharing is ubiquitous; shared information lives on "servers."
Computer networking	Load-sharing among a modest number of major computers	Electronic mail; widespread sharing of software and data; local area networks (the original networks were wide-area); the interconnection of literally millions of computers	Networking has enabled worldwide communication and sharing, access to expertise wherever it exists, and commerce at our fingertips.
Workstations	Enough computing to make interactive graphic useful	Displaced most other forms of computing and terminals; led directly to personal computers and multimedia	Millions in use for science, engineering, and finance
Computer graphics	Make pictures on a computer.	"What you see is what you get" and hypermedia documents	Almost any image is possible. Realistic moving images made on computers are routinely seen on television and were used effectively in the design of the Boeing 777.
"Windows and mouse" user interface technology	Easy access to many applications and documents at once	Dramatic improvements in overall ease of use; the integration of applications (e.g., spreadsheets, word processors, and presentation graphics)	The standard way to use all computers
Very large integrated circuit design	New design methods to keep pace with integrated circuit technology	Easy access to "silicon foundries"; a renaissance in computer design	Many more schools training VLSI designers; many more companies using this technology
Reduced Instruction Set Computers (RISC)	Computers 2 to 3 times faster	Dramatic progress in the "co-design" of hardware and software, leading to significantly greater performance	Millions in use; penetration continues to increase
Redundant Arrays of Inexpensive Disks (RAID)	Faster, more reliable disk systems	RAID is more economical as well: massive data repositories ride the price/performance wave of personal computers and workstations.	Entering the mainstream for large-scale data storage; will see widespread commercial use in digital video servers

continues

TABLE 1.1—*continued*

Topic	Goal	Unanticipated Results	Today
Parallel computing	Significantly faster computing to address complex problems	Parallel deskside server system; unanticipated applications such as transaction processing, financial modeling, database mining, and knowledge discovery in data	Many computer manufacturers include parallel computing as a standard offering.
Digital libraries	Universal, multimedia (text, image, audio, video) access to all the information in large libraries; an essential need is tools for discovering and locating information	Pending development	Beginning development

From this record of success we can draw some important conclusions:

• *Research pays off for an extended period.* The federal investment and the payoff, including the spawning of numerous corporations and multibillion-dollar industries, have been continuous for decades.

• *Unanticipated results are often the most important results.* Information sharing is an unanticipated result of timesharing; what-you-see-is-what-you-get displays and hypermedia documents are unanticipated results of computer graphics; electronic mail is an unanticipated result of networking.

• *The fusion of ideas multiplies their effect.* Distributed systems, such as automated teller machine networks, combine elements of timesharing, networking, workstations, and computer graphics. Personal digital assistants, the emerging generation of truly portable computers, combine these elements with new networking and power-management technologies.

• *Research trains people.* A major output of publicly supported research programs has been people. Some develop or create a new concept and start companies to commercialize their knowledge. Others form a pool of expertise that allows new or existing companies to move quickly into new technologies.

• *The synergy among industry, academia, and government has been highly effective.* The flow of ideas and people between government-sponsored and commercial programs is suggested in Figure 1.2.

BOX 1.2 An Example of a Successful
Federal R&D Program: The ARPA VLSI Program

The ARPA VLSI program began in the late 1970s. This program, inspired by the ground-breaking work of Carver Mead and Lynn Conway, envisioned that integrated circuit technology could be made available to system designers and that this would have tremendous impact. The program funded academic research activities as well as the Metal Oxide Semiconductor Implemention Service (MOSIS). MOSIS provided low-cost, fast-turnaround VLSI fabrication services to the research community; established by ARPA, it was expanded and had access broadened by the National Science Foundation. The ARPA VLSI program is widely regarded to have been a tremendous success. Among its notable achievements are the following:

- Developed the concept of the multichip wafer, which allowed multiple designs to share a single silicon fabrication run. Together with tools developed to assemble the designs and provide services for digital submission of chip designs, this capability made the concept of a low-cost, fast-turnaround silicon foundry a reality. Several companies were formed based on these ideas, with VLSI Technology Inc. being the best known.

- Stimulated development of the Geometry Engine and Pixel Planes projects, which used the capabilities of VLSI to create new capabilities in low-cost, high-performance three-dimensional graphics. The Geometry Engine project formed the basis of Silicon Graphics Inc. Pixel planes technology is licensed to Ivex and Division.

- Stimulated development of Berkeley UNIX, which was funded to provide a research platform for the VLSI design tools. This version of UNIX eventually became the basis for the operating system of choice in workstations, servers, and multiprocessors. UNIX went on to become the most widely used vendor-independent operating system, with the code developed at Berkeley being key to this development.

- Accelerated understanding of the importance of low-cost, high-quality graphics for VLSI design, inspiring the creation of the Stanford University Network (SUN) workstation project. Together with the UNIX development from Berkeley, this technology formed the basis for Sun Microsystems.

- Developed two of the three RISC experiments, the Berkeley RISC project and the Stanford MIPS project, which were major parts of the VLSI program inspired by the possibilities of VLSI technology. These technologies formed the basis for many RISC designs, including those of MIPS Computer Systems (now owned by Silicon Graphics Inc.) and Sun Microsystems.

- Sponsored extensive developments in computer-aided design (CAD) tool design. These led to revolutionary improvements in CAD technology for layout, design rule checking, and simulation. The tools developed in this program were used extensively in both academic research programs and in industry. The ideas were developed in commercial implementations by companies such as VLSI Technology, Cadnetix, and more recently, Synopsis.

Overall, the ARPA VLSI program was a landmark success, not only in creating new technologies and revolutionizing the computer industry, but also in forming the basis for major new industrial technologies and a number of companies that have become major corporations.*

---

*Interestingly, the success of the ARPA VLSI program stands in sharp contrast to the Department of Defense VHSIC program, which based entirely in industry and is generally regarded to have had only modest impact either in developing new technologies or in accelerating technology.

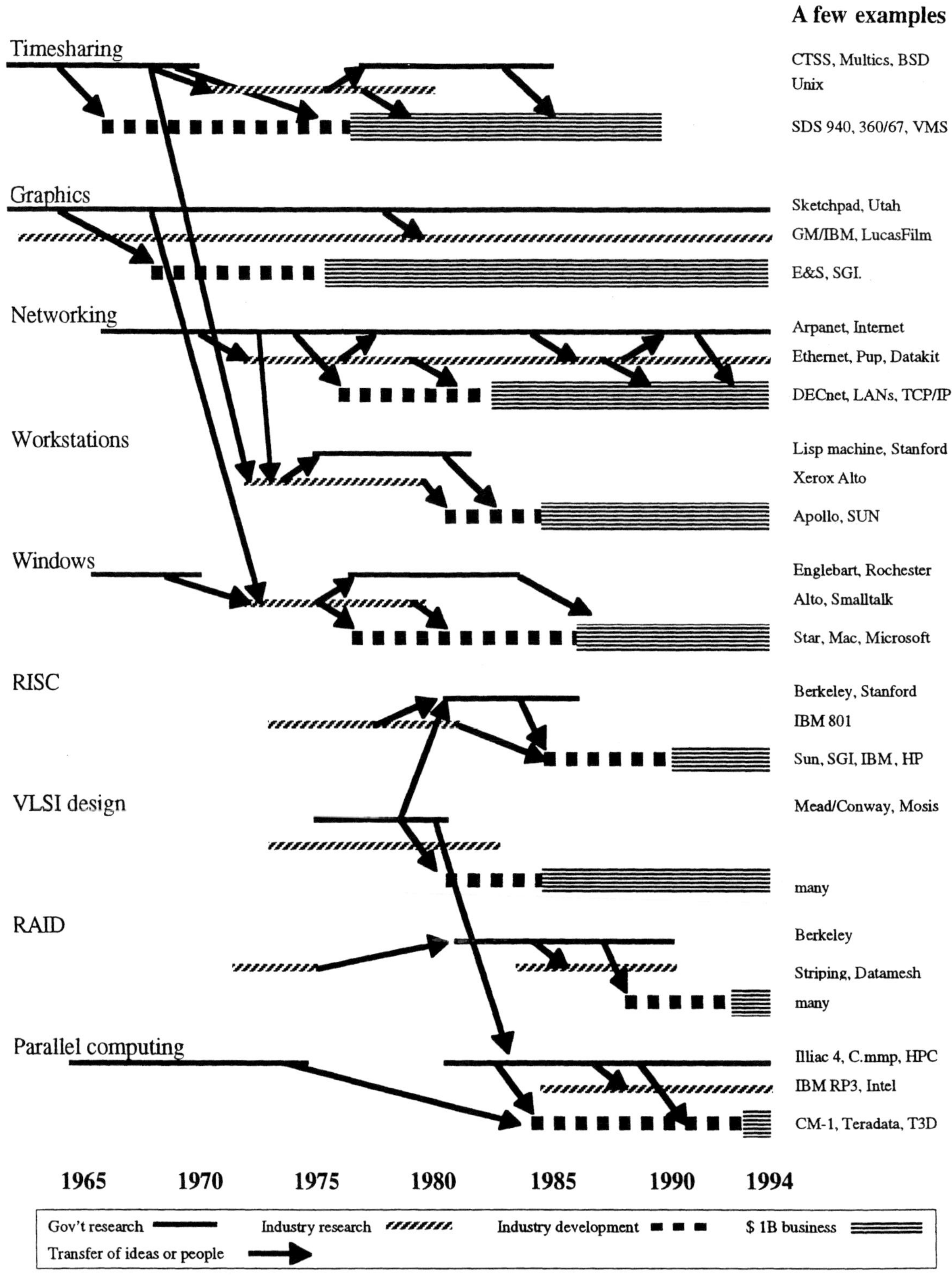

FIGURE 1.2 Government-sponsored computing research and development stimulates creation of innovative ideas and industries. Dates apply to horizontal bars, but not to arrows showing transfer of ideas and people. Table 1.1 is a companion to this figure.

BOX 1.3 An Example of the Impact of Federal R&D Support in Establishing a Field: Computer Graphics

In the middle 1960s, using a computer on loan from the Air Force and financial support from the Central Intelligence Agency, the computer graphics group at Harvard University demonstrated a prototype virtual reality system. This work contributed significantly to the technological and personnel foundation for the Evans and Sutherland Corporation, which subsequently provided computer-based equipment for training pilots—equipment that is used today by the U.S. military and by commercial pilots the world over.

In the early 1970s the University of Utah was host to a leading program in computer graphics. Dave Evans went there to found a computer science department, and realizing that his department could not be all things to all people, he specialized in computer graphics. ARPA provided the main research support.

At that time nearly all pictures of three-dimensional objects were drawn with lines only. The resulting images appeared to be of wire frames. They were not very realistic. The Utah group worked mainly on techniques for increasing the realism by omitting parts of objects that were hidden behind other parts and by shading the surfaces of the objects. The resulting pictures were much more realistic.

Two key developments had particularly significant impact. First, Watkins and others, following a suggestion of Evans, developed a set of incremental techniques for computing what parts of an object were hidden. The key observation was that two parts of the image must be nearly the same if they are close together. When some part of an image has been computed, nearby parts are easier to compute than they would be if computed in isolation.

Second, Gouraud and Phong and others developed incremental algorithms for shading solid surfaces. Prior to their work the best images appeared to be made with flat surfaces; each surface was painted a single shade according to the angle between it, the light, and the observer. Many workers sought methods for representing objects with curved surfaces, but it was then and is still difficult. Instead, Gouraud invented a trick. He painted each surface a gradually changing shade in such a way that at the joints between surfaces they had the same shade. With no demarcation line, the human eye thinks the resulting surface is smooth even though it is made of little flat plates. Phong went a step further, computing highlights as if the surface were curved. Gouraud shading and Phong shading are in standard use everywhere today. It is particularly interesting to note that when government support started, no one knew that these technologies were possible and the people who made the key discoveries were not yet involved.

The vast implications of computer graphics (what-you-see-is-what-you-get document creation systems, scientific visualization, the entertainment industry, virtual reality) were of course totally unforeseen at the time that this fundamental research was undertaken. In addition to the specific developments cited above, an essential contribution was the many individuals whose training in universities benefited from ARPA support. A few of the more prominent are John Warnock of Adobe Systems ($300 million per year), Jim Clark (formerly) of Silicon Graphics Inc. ($1 billion per year), Henry Fuchs of the University of North Carolina, and Ed Catmull of Pixar. Many others carried the knowledge to companies and academic institutions throughout the nation.

• *Even for defense applications, supporting research on strategically motivated but broadly applicable computing and communications technology has clearly been the right approach.* In the past, many defense applications and requirements presaged commercial applications and requirements. Today, commercial computer systems and applications often find use in defense environments.

• *Research and development take time.* At least 10 years, more often 15, elapse between initial research and commercial success. This is true even for research of strategic importance. And it is true in spite of the rapid pace of today's product development, as indicated in the timeline for recent commercial successes such as RISC and windows (see Figure 1.2).

BOX 1.4 Federal R&D Support Propels Database Technology

The database industry generated about $7 billion in revenue in 1994 and is growing at a rate of 35 percent per year. All database industry leaders are U.S.-based corporations: IBM, Oracle, Sybase, Informix, Computer Associates, and Microsoft. In addition, there are two large specialty vendors, both also U.S.-based: Tandem, selling over $1 billion per year of fault-tolerant transaction processing systems, and AT&T-Teradata, selling about $500 million per year of data mining systems. In addition to these well-established companies, there is a vibrant group of small companies specializing in application-specific databases, object-oriented databases, and desktop databases.

A very modest federal research investment, complemented by a modest industrial research investment, led directly to U.S. dominance of this market. It is not possible to list all the contributions here, but three representative research projects are highlighted that had major impact on the industry.

1. Project Ingres started at the University of California, Berkeley, in 1972. Inspired by Codd's landmark paper on relational databases, several faculty members (Stonebraker, Rowe, Wong, and others) started a project to design and build a system. Incidental to this work, they invented a query language (QUEL), relational optimization techniques, a language binding technique, and interesting storage strategies. They also pioneered work on distributed databases.

The Ingres academic system formed the basis for the Ingres product now owned by Computer Associates. Students trained on Ingres went on to start or staff all the major database companies (AT&T, Britton Lee, HP, Informix, IBM, Oracle, Tandem, Sybase). The Ingres project went on to investigate distributed databases, database inference, active databases, and extensible databases. It was rechristened Postgres, which is now the basis of the digital library and scientific database efforts within the University of California system. Recently, Postgres spun off to become the basis for a new object-relational system from the start-up Illustra Information Technologies.

2. System R was IBM Research's response to Codd's ideas. His relational model was at first very controversial; people thought that the model was too simplistic and that it would never perform well. IBM Research management took a gamble and chartered a small (10-person) effort to prototype a relational system based on Codd's ideas. That effort produced a prototype, System R, that eventually grew into the DB2 product series. Along the way, the IBM team pioneered ideas in query optimization, data independence (views), transactions (logging and locking), and security (the grant-revoke model). In addition, the SQL query language from System R was the basis for the ANSI/ISO standard.

The System R group went on to investigate distributed databases (project R*) and object-oriented extensible databases (project Starburst). These research projects have pioneered new ideas and algorithms. The results appear in IBM's database products and those of other vendors.

3. The University of Wisconsin's Gamma system was a highly successful effort that prototyped a high-performance parallel database system built of off-the-shelf system components.

During the 1970s there had been great enthusiasm for database machines—special-purpose computers that would be much faster than general-purpose systems running conventional databases. These research projects were often based on exotic hardware like bubble memories, head-per-track disks, or associative random access memory. The problem was that general-purpose systems were improving at a rate of 50 percent per year, and so it was difficult for exotic systems to compete with them. By 1980, most researchers realized the futility of special-purpose approaches, and the database machine community switched to research on using arrays of general-purpose processors and disks to process data in parallel.

The University of Wisconsin was home to the major proponents of this idea in the United States. Funded by government and industry, researchers prototyped and built a parallel database machine called Gamma, whose hardware base was an early Intel scalable parallel machine. That system produced ideas and a generation of students who went on to staff all the database vendors. Today, the highly successful parallel database systems from IBM, Tandem, Oracle, Informix, Sybase, and AT&T all have a direct lineage from the Wisconsin research on parallel database systems. The use of parallel databases systems for data mining is now the fastest-growing component of the database server industry.

The Gamma project evolved into the Exodus project at Wisconsin (focusing on an extensible object-oriented database). Exodus has now evolved to the Paradise system, which combines object-oriented and parallel database techniques to represent, store, and quickly process huge Earth-observing satellite databases.

SOURCE: James Gray and others for the Computing Research Association; reproduced with permission.

CONTINUED FEDERAL INVESTMENT IS NECESSARY TO SUSTAIN OUR LEAD

What must be done to sustain the innovation and growth needed for enhancing the information infrastructure and maintaining U.S. leadership in information technology? Rapid and continuing change in the technology, a 10- to 15-year cycle from idea to commercial success, and successive waves of new companies are characteristics of the information industry that point to the need for a stable source of expertise and some room for a long-term approach. Three observations seem pertinent.

1. *Industrial R&D cannot replace government investment in basic research.* Very few companies are able to invest for a payoff that is 10 years away. Moreover, many advances are broad in their applicability and complex enough to take several engineering iterations to get right, and so the key insights become "public" and a single company cannot recoup the research investment. Public investment in research that creates a reservoir of new ideas and trained people is repaid many times over by jobs and taxes in the information industry, more innovation and productivity in other industries, and improvements in the daily lives of citizens. This investment is essential to maintain U.S. international competitiveness.

Of course, industrial R&D also contributes to the nation's pool of new ideas, but a company may postpone exploiting its ideas if they disturb existing business. A good example is the evolution of RISC processors shown in Figure 1.2. RISC was invented by John Cocke, an IBM researcher, but IBM made no RISC products for a decade. Only after the ideas were embraced and extended in government-sponsored work at universities did industry adopt them, and this adoption was initiated by young companies, including Sun Microsystems, and start-ups, including MIPS. Now, a decade later, IBM is one of the leaders in exploiting RISC technology, but the cost to IBM of this delay has been significant. Firms have regularly failed to adapt to change as evidenced by the departure from the computer business of GE, RCA, Honeywell, Philco, Perkin-Elmer, Control Data, and Prime; the folding together by merger of other manufacturers; and major downsizing at IBM and DEC. It often is easier for a start-up to form, raise venture capital, and succeed than for an established firm to abandon a currently successful direction in favor of a new approach just when the old approach is most financially successful. Even in a vigorous industrial R&D climate, then, federal investment in research is necessary, both for its long-term focus and for its ability to incubate ideas to the point of clear commercial viability.

But the need for federal investment in research is further compounded by the fact that industrial R&D is already under stress. In the computing hardware and software sector, for example, although a small number of new R&D enterprises have been launched, most notably by Microsoft, there has been a general consolidation of resources by companies such as IBM and DEC, including an apparent reduction in their research effort or at least a greater emphasis on short-term R&D—a change in emphasis is evident to insiders and close observers but not easy to document.[5] The industry-wide level of R&D as a percentage of sales has also been brought down by the tendency of low-price vendors, such as Dell and Gateway, to ride on the research conducted by others.

The trend toward reduced industrial R&D appears also in the telecommunications industry. The 1984 divestiture of AT&T led to a smaller Bell Laboratories and to the creation of Bell Communications Research (Bellcore), a shared research facility for the seven regional Bell holding companies. Recent deregulation has encouraged a reduction of basic research at both AT&T and Bellcore. Lacking significant research capability at its individual service companies, the cable television industry depends on research done by its hardware vendors and its shared CableLabs. Although more new technology has been deployed in telecommunications since deregulation in the early 1980s, and although in both computing and communications there are more companies selling products now than there were 15 years ago, today's sales are based on yesterday's research and do not guarantee a sufficient foundation for tomorrow's sales. Competition in an industry can promote technological growth, but competition alone is not the source of innovation and leadership.

Because of the long time scales involved in research, the full effect of decreasing investment in research may not be evident for a decade, but by then, it may be too late to reverse an erosion of research capability. Thus, even though many private-sector organizations that have weighed in on one or more policy areas relating to the enhancement of information infrastructure typically argue for a minimal government role in commercialization, they tend to support a continuing federal presence in relevant basic research.[6]

2. *It is hard to predict which new ideas and approaches will succeed.* Over the years, federal support of computing and communications research in universities has helped make possible an environment for exploration and experimentation, leading to a broad range of diverse ideas from which the marketplace ultimately has selected winners and losers. As demonstrated by the unforeseen applications and results listed in Table 1.1, it is difficult to know in advance the outcome or final value of a particular line of inquiry. But the history of development in computing and communications suggests that innovation arises from a diversity of ideas and some freedom to take a long-range view. It is notoriously difficult to place a specific value on the generation of knowledge and experience, but such benefits are much broader than sales of specific systems.

3. *Research and development in information technology can make good use of equipment that is 10 years in advance of current "commodity" practice.* When it is first used for research, such a piece of equipment is often a supercomputer. By the time that research makes its way to commercial use, computers of equal power are no longer expensive or rare. For example, the computer graphics techniques that are available on desktop workstations today, and that will soon be on personal computers and set-top boxes, were pioneered on the multimillion-dollar supercomputers of the 1960s and 1970s. Part of the task in information technology R&D is to find out how today's supercomputers can be used when they are cheap and widely available, and thus to feed the industries of tomorrow.

The large-scale systems problems presented both by massive parallelism and by massive information infrastructure are additional distinguishing characteristics of information systems R&D, because they imply a need for scale in the research effort itself. In principle, collaborative efforts might help to overcome the problem of attaining critical mass and scale, yet history suggests that there are relatively few collaborations in basic research within any industry, and purely industrial (and increasingly industry-university or industry-government) collaborations tend to disseminate results more slowly than university-based research.

The government-supported research program (on the order of $1 billion for information technology R&D) is small compared to industrial R&D (on the order of $20 billion; Coy, 1993), but it constitutes a significant portion of the research component, and it is a critical factor because it supports the exploratory work that is difficult for industry to afford, allows the pursuit of ideas that may lead to success in unexpected ways, and nourishes the industry of the future, creating jobs and benefits for ourselves and our children. The industrial R&D investment, though larger in dollars, is different in nature: it focuses on the near term—increasingly so, as noted earlier—and is thus vulnerable to major opportunity costs. The increasing tendency to focus on the near term is affecting the body of the nation's overall R&D. Despite economic studies showing that the United States leads the world in reaping benefits from basic research, pressures in all sectors appear to be promoting a shift in universities toward near-term efforts, resulting in a decline in basic research even as a share of university research (Cohen and Noll, 1994). Thus, a general reduction in support for basic research appears to be taking place.

It is critical to understand that there are dramatic new opportunities that still can be developed by fundamental research in information technology—opportunities on which the nation must capitalize. These include high-performance systems and applications for science and engineering; high-confidence systems for applications such as health care, law enforcement, and finance; building blocks for global-scale information utilities (e.g., electronic payment); interactive environments for applications ranging from telemedicine to entertainment; improved user interfaces to allow the creation and use of ever more sophisticated applications by ever broader cross sections of the population; and the creation of the human capital on which the next generation's information industries will be based. Fundamental research in computing and communications is the key to unlocking the potential of these new applications.

How much federal research support is proper for the foreseeable future and to what aspects of information technology should it be devoted?[7] Answering this question is part of a larger process of considering how to reorient overall federal spending on R&D from a context dominated by national security to one driven more by other economic and social goals. It is harder to achieve the kind of consensus needed to sustain federal research programs associated with these goals than it was under the national security aegis. Nevertheless, the fundamental rationale for federal programs remains (Cohen and Noll, 1994, p. 73):

> That R&D can enhance the nation's economic welfare is not, by itself, sufficient reason to justify a prominent role for the federal government in financing it. Economists have developed a further rationale for government subsidies. Their consensus is that most of the benefits of innovation accrue not to innovators but to consumers through products that are better or less expensive, or both. Because the benefits of technological progress are broadly shared, innovators lack the financial incentive to improve technologies as much as is socially desirable. Therefore, the government can improve the performance of the economy by adopting policies that facilitate and increase investments in research.

TODAY THE HPCCI IS THE UMBRELLA FOR MOST GOVERNMENT-SPONSORED COMPUTING AND COMMUNICATIONS RESEARCH

Today, the HPCCI is the umbrella sheltering most government-sponsored computing and communications research. The HPCCI is thus responsible for sustaining the nation's lead in information technology. It centers on rising performance as the driver for progress across a wide range of technologies.

"High performance" means bringing a large quantity of computing and communications to bear on one problem. It is far broader than "supercomputing," which was the focus of early public policy in this area. It is also a moving target—the threshold for what is considered "high performance" advances, as ever-increasing performance levels become more broadly available. The supercomputer of this generation is the group server of the next generation and the personal computer of the generation after that. The same is true for communications: today's leading edge is tomorrow's mainstream.

Focusing research on the leading edge of performance accelerates the broad availability of what starts out as limited-access technology, in the following ways:

• *By advancing the hardware and software systems themselves.* Many techniques now used to build mainstream computers and their software were originally developed for high-performance computing: specialized floating-point processing, pipelining, multiprocessing, and multiple instruction issue, among others;

• *By creating new applications today so that they will be mature when the hardware that can run them is cheap and ubiquitous.* It can take much longer to develop and fully exploit a new application than to build a new computer. Overcoming this lag is one of the drivers of work on the Grand and National Challenge concepts; and

• *By attacking problems that would otherwise be beyond reach for several years, thus speeding up the development of new fields of science, engineering, medicine, and business.* National access to machines with 100 to 1,000 times the memory and speed of researchers' desktop machines allows them to make qualitative jumps to exploring frontier research problems of higher dimensionality, greater resolution, or more complexity than would otherwise be possible.

Fundamental but strategic research under the HPCCI—which now encompasses most of the academic computing research sponsored by the federal government—creates a strong pull on the computer science and engineering research community, the user community, and the hardware, software, and telecommunications vendors. For example, it was evident to individuals in the computing and communications research community that as VLSI circuit technology developed, it would favor computing structures based on the large-scale replication of modest processors, as opposed to the small-scale replication of processors of the highest attainable individual performance. (The highest-speed circuits are expensive to design, produce, maintain, and operate.) This vision of high-performance computing and communications based on parallelism brought three major technical challenges: (1) interconnection and memory architecture—how to unite large numbers of relatively inexpensive processors into systems capable of delivering truly high performance, and (2) programming—how to program such collections of processors to solve large and complex problems. In the networking arena, the obvious issues of large-scale, widespread use and high-speed transmission were compounded by added problems of connecting heterogeneous systems and achieving high reliability.

The technical and economic imperatives that led to the HPCCI are discussed in some detail in Appendix A. HPCCI was, and continues to be, an appropriate thrust. As Chapter 2 discusses, the HPCCI can boast a broad range of very significant accomplishments. However, the committee sees an unhealthy dependence of our nation's critical leadership in information technology on the fate of a single initiative. First, not all important computing research is focused on high performance, although the politics of funding have encouraged researchers and agencies to paint everything with an HPCCI brush. Second, we cannot afford to cripple computing research if the nation's attention and resources turn away from any single goal. At the beginning of the HPCCI in 1992, its increasing momentum made association with it attractive and helped the initiative attain both intellectual and financial critical mass. The rise of the National Information Infrastructure initiative, though, underscores how changeable the federal funding process may be.

We must move toward a more mature approach in which a substantial focus on goals of obvious national importance is combined with a diversified program of long-term exploration of important research problems that support the strategic information technology industry. We can change the HPCCI's name, we can change its orientation, but we must move forward. Continuing the momentum of this successful initiative is essential to ongoing U.S. prosperity and leadership in information technology.

NOTES

1. Microcomputers (personal computers) are defined as computers with a list price of $1,000 to $14,999; see CBEMA (1994), pp. 60-61. Forrester (1994, pp. 2-3) estimates the share of households with PCs at about 20 percent, based on their survey of households and Bureau of Census data. Forrester's model accounts for retirements of older PCs and for households with multiple PCs. This is a lower estimate than the Software Publishing Association's widely cited 30 percent share. Building on an unusual fourth quarter sales surge, almost 7 million PCs were sold for residential use in 1994 (Markoff, 1995). According to another source, fourth quarter 1994 U.S. PC shipments were 32 percent higher than the corresponding quarter in 1993, 5.8 million units, feeding a 27 percent surge in worldwide PC shipments for 1994 in total (Carlton, 1994).

2. According to Roach (1994, p. 12), "IT [information technology] expenditures now comprise fully 45 percent of total business outlays on capital equipment—easily the largest line item in Corporate America's investment budget and up dramatically from a 20% share seen as recently as 1980 . . . . But does the technology story have staying power? We believe that the new dynamics of technology demand should continue to power the U.S. economy throughout the 1990s. Indeed, *the technology-capital-spending link is an integral element of the productivity-led recovery scenario that lies at the heart of our basic macro call for the United States* [emphasis in original]. In this light, IT is the principal means by which businesses can improve upon the efficiency gains first derived from cost-cutting, facilitating the transition between slash-and-burn downsizing and the rebuilding eventually required for sustained competitive prowess. Without increasing emphasis on technology, the economy gets hollowed out. The good news is that the long-awaited technology payback suggests this darker scenario won't come to pass."

3. See U.S. DOC (1994); the Department of Commerce utilizes data from the U.S. Bureau of the Census series, the *Annual Survey of Manufactures*. It places the value of shipments for the information technology industry at $421 billion for 1993. This number omits revenue from equipment rentals, fees for after-sale service, and markups in the product distribution channel. It also excludes office equipment in total. It includes computers, storage devices, terminals, and peripherals; packaged software; computer program manufacturing, data processing, information services, facilities management, and other services; and telecommunications equipment and services.

See also CBEMA (1994); CBEMA values the worldwide 1993 revenue of the U.S. information technology industry at $602 billion. In addition to including office equipment, it shows larger revenues for information technology hardware and telecommunications equipment than does the Department of Commerce.

4. In addition, European and Japanese manufacturers have significant sales in computer-related products such as telecommunications switches, semiconductors, and even high-performance computing equipment.

5. See Rensberger (1994) and Corcoran (1994). Also Coy (1993) indicates that data on individual information technology companies show 1992 R&D spending as a percent of sales ranging from 1 to 15 percent, concentrated at the lower end of that range; industry segment statistics fall in the same range. The figures suggest that despite the "high-tech" image of the industry, less R&D is conducted than many believe, and many firms capitalize on research conducted by others.

6. See, for example, CSPP (1994), pp. 1-2. A broad argument for a federal role in support of basic research in critical technologies, including computing and communications, is presented in a Council on Competitiveness (1991) report.

7. A point of reference can be found in a mid-1994 document from the Electronics Subcommittee of the National Science and Technology Council (NSTC, 1994a). It calls attention to U.S. dependence on a healthy electronics industry and speaks of efforts to work with industry to "develop a roadmap for electronics that will illuminate gaps in government-sponsored research and infrastructure efforts," focusing on "information products that connect to information networks, including the National Information Infrastructure (NII)."

2
The High Performance Computing and Communications Initiative

The High Performance Computing and Communications Initiative (HPCCI) has been the focal point of federal support for U.S. computing and communications research and development since 1989. It became official in 1991 with Office of Science and Technology Policy (OSTP) support and enactment of the High Performance Computing Act of 1991. It includes five programs: Advanced Software Technology and Algorithms, Basic Research and Human Resources (although there is basic research in the other four programs also), High-Performance Computing Systems, National Research and Education Network (NREN), and since FY 1994, Information Infrastructure Technology and Applications (IITA).[1] Appendix A outlines the origins and early history of the HPCCI, including an explanation of associated technology trends and indications of evolution of the initiative's emphases. This chapter discusses the HPCCI's goals and contributions to date and identifies key substantive and practical issues to be considered as the initiative evolves.[2]

HPCCI: GOALS AND EMPHASES

The HPCCI has several broad goals (NCO, 1993):

- Extend U.S. leadership in high-performance computing and networking technologies;
- Disseminate the technologies to accelerate innovation and serve the economy, national security, education, and the environment; and
- Spur gains in U.S. productivity and industrial competitiveness.

Because these goals relate advances in computing and communications technologies to the achievement of benefits from their use, the HPCCI has from its inception provided for the joint advancement of technologies and applications. The HPCCI has pursued several specific strategic objectives.

Basic Objectives

Teraflop Capability

The specific objective for computer development was to develop teraflop capability by the mid-1990s.[3] This objective was comparable to two that had been achieved earlier by forerunners of today's computer science community at the request of the federal government: peak available computing power was increased by several orders of magnitude during World War II, when federal interests in cryptanalysis and other wartime needs led to the development of the vacuum tube computer, and in the late 1950s, when federal interests in military command and control led to transistorized computers.[4] As economist Kenneth Flamm has observed, "By tracking the origins and history of key pieces of technology, a simple but important point can be established: at certain, crucial moments in history, private commercial interests, in the absence of government support, would not have become as intensely involved in certain long-term basic research and radical new concepts" (Flamm, 1988, p. 3). The teraflop objective has inspired parallel multi-microprocessor computers as the means for providing the next major jump in computer power.[5]

The teraflop objective has generated both attention and misunderstanding. Progress required building a number of machines large and fast enough to reward software researchers and application users with major gains in performance, thereby motivating them to develop the code that could make the high-performance machines useful. (See Appendix A for more information on the development of high-performance hardware and software and their interaction.) The costliness of this undertaking, compounded by the highly publicized financial difficulties of two entrepreneurial ventures, Thinking Machines Corporation (TMC) and Kendall Square Research (KSR), aimed at commercializing massively parallel computing systems, attracted criticism of the HPCCI.

However, that criticism appears largely misdirected. First, entrepreneurial ventures are always risky, and the two in question suffered from managerial weakness at least as much as questionable technology choices.[6] Contemporaneously, more established firms (e.g., Cray Research, IBM, Intel Supercomputing, Convex Computer, and Silicon Graphics Inc.; Parker-Smith, 1994a) have persevered, and others (e.g., Hitachi and NEC in Japan; Kahaner, 1994b, and Parker-Smith, 1994b) have entered or expanded their presence in the parallel systems market. Second, focusing attention on the high initial costs for stimulating development and use of parallel processing systems detracts from the achievement of successful proofs of concept and dissemination of new approaches to computation.

Although the teraflop objective was ambitious for the time scale set, it was intended as a driver and thus is best viewed as indicating a direction, not a destination; the need for progress in computing will continue beyond the teraflop capability.[7] In that respect, its appropriateness was affirmed by the 1993 Branscomb panel.[8] The teraflop objective has, in fact, served to focus attention on the task of combining and harnessing vast amounts of computer power from many smaller computers. The technology is now sufficiently developed that a teraflop machine could be realized today, although exactly when to do so should be left to the economics of users and their applications.[9]

High-speed Networks

Another direction-setting objective of the HPCCI was the achievement of data communications networks attaining speeds of at least 1 gigabit per second. Although by the mid-1980s major telecommunications networks already had gigabit-plus trunk circuits in their backbones, the HPCCI was intended to lead to much broader deployment of and access to gigabit-speed networks connecting general-purpose computers.[10] This objective drove progress in switching, computing hardware and software, interfaces, and communication protocols.[11] (See Appendix B.)

Grand Challenges

A third original objective related to applications of high-performance computing and communications technologies: to define and attack Grand Challenge problems. High-performance computing and communications national centers in the various agencies already were providing access to tens of thousands of researchers in hundreds of institutions when the HPCCI began. Drawing from this national base of users, various HPCCI agencies have defined a series of Grand Challenge problems (see Appendix D for list) and chosen teams to attack them. The Grand Challenge teams are typically both interdisciplinary and multi-institutional. The scientific problems are picked for their intrinsic scientific merit, the need for high-performance computation and communications, the opportunities for synergistic interaction of computer scientists with computational scientists, and the scientific and societal benefits to be gained from their solution. For example, better weather prediction involves solving massive sets of equations, experimenting with models, and comparing the results obtained with them to increasingly large volumes of data collected by weather-monitoring instruments.[12] High-performance computing provides the faster model computation essential to timely assessment of a sufficiently large volume of alternative weather patterns for a given period (e.g., a month).[13] The results include not only greater scientific understanding, but also the benefits to businesses, individuals, and governments that come from faster, more accurate, and more detailed forecasts.

Expanded Objectives

The set of HPCCI objectives has been expanded through legislative and agency activities. The High Performance Computing Act of 1991, Public Law 102-194, broadened the applications concerns to include the so-called National Challenges—explorations of high-performance computing and communications technology for applications in such areas as education, libraries, manufacturing, and health care. PL 102-194 also reinforced the communications aspects of the HPCCI, elaborating the concept and objectives for the NREN program and emphasizing networking applications in education. Officials involved with the HPCCI have noted that although PL 102-194 was never complemented by specific appropriations legislation, its principles have driven HPCCI activities in relevant agencies, including early explorations relating to National Challenges and the formation of the Information Infrastructure Technology and Applications (IITA) component in FY 1994.[14] The National Challenges, IITA, and the network aspects of PL 102-194 also included attention to short-term and practical concerns (e.g., expanding access to technology facilities and capabilities), complementing the long-term, basic research problems that remain at the heart of HPCCI.[15]

The tension between long term and short term, between basic research and applications, is fundamental to the differences in opinion voiced about the HPCCI and its merits, accomplishments, and desired directions. Based on its direct observations of work funded under the HPCCI and on its discussions with others in universities, industry, and the government, the committee affirms the value of the basic research associated with the HPCCI, research that is informed by needs associated with important applications of national interest.

A fundamental issue shaping the evolution of the HPCCI is the balance to be struck between the support of applications that use high-performance computing and communications technologies and the support for computer science research on new high-performance computing and communications technologies.[16] The committee's analysis of the FY 1995 HPCCI budget request (Appendix C) shows that out of the total request of $1.15 billion, $352 million (30 percent) would be invested in basic research in computer, software, or communication technologies; $205 million (18 percent) in applied computer science research in common applications support, artificial intelligence, and human-machine interface; $176 million (15 percent) in direct support of applications and computational science; and $297 million (26 percent) in supercomputing and communications infrastructure. It is hard to interpret these statistics, however, without an understanding of the nature and the value of the work labeled "applications." The HPCCI has been aimed at catalyzing a paradigm shift, which involves the synergistic interaction of people developing the technology and people using the technology.[17] The HPCCI includes mission-related activities that may drive computing and communications research and development (R&D) and/or applications that call for significant technology development.

Within the computer science and engineering field, there has been considerable debate over the degree to which computing research should be driven by applications concerns as opposed to intrinsic computer science concerns, given that both approaches to research have historically yielded considerable spinoffs to other sciences and the economy.[18] To computer scientists and engineers, HPCCI is viewed as the first major federal initiative that emphasizes the science of computing and communications, which is addressed in conjunction with exploration of problems involving other fields of science and engineering, loosely aggregated as computational science. To computational scientists, the emphasis is predictably on the problems in their domains and on the difficulty of developing appropriate domain-specific computational techniques. These differences in outlook result in differences in what each community calls an "application," as well as differences in requirements for R&D.

HPCCI ACCOMPLISHMENTS

Accomplishments under the HPCCI to date reveal two key trends: better computing and computational infrastructure and increasing researcher-developer-user synergy. In the committee's expert judgment, HPCCI has been generally successful. That assessment is necessarily qualitative and experiential, because it is too early yet to observe the full impact of the initiative.

The Issue of Measurement

Early measurement of the impact of HPCCI research is problematic. As Chapter 1 points out, the time for progress from idea to product involves a decade or more, well beyond a single fiscal year. Independent of impact, individual projects may take a few years simply to reach completion.[19] Consequently, the accomplishments of the HPCCI are only just becoming apparent.

Moreover, it is difficult to evaluate early on how good individual ideas are and what their worth may prove to be. Many researchers have expressed concern that the push for immediately measurable results has led to an unrealistic emphasis on short-term gains and has diverted efforts from conducting productive research to maintaining "paper trails."[20] However, the pressures on agencies to maximize the return on limited research funds seems to discourage funding of more innovative—and therefore riskier—exploration that may not necessarily succeed (Rensberger, 1994). The problem of measurement is compounded by the fact that a considerable amount of HPCCI research addresses enabling technologies whose benefits or outcomes may be evident only indirectly.

How best to assess results is unclear—key questions include the kinds of reviews already undertaken by agencies and with what effect; how evaluations based on outside expertise should be combined with in-house agency know-how; whether to focus on reviewing progress for a program as a whole or progress in individual grants; the costs in time and money of different approaches and comparison of the benefits in terms of review quality, scope, and timeliness to the costs; and so on. The committee recognizes that data and analysis are needed to support decision making about any new approaches to evaluation; it did not have the time or resources to pursue such analysis.[21] Moreover, complementing the committee's observation that much of the evidence on outcomes is anecdotal is a recent National Research Council study pointing out that good, relevant data (on scientific research in general) are hard to find and even harder to draw inferences from (CPSMA, 1994).

Better Computing and Computational Infrastructure

The HPCCI has contributed substantially to the development, deployment, and understanding of computing and communications facilities and capabilities as infrastructure. It has helped transform understanding of how to share resources and information, generating proofs of concept and understanding that are of value not only to the scientific research community but also to the economy and society at large.

The HPCCI has directly strengthened academic computing and computational infrastructure, building on the National Science Foundation's (NSF's) significant investments in university computing infrastructure over more than a decade.[22] The NSF infrastructure program has stimulated complementary investments by other federal agencies, industry, and universities themselves—an impact that, like other HPCCI contributions to stimulating a growing foundation of activity, is difficult to assess directly. This academic base, in particular, academic research in experimental computer science and engineering,[23] is fundamental to the development and application of high-performance and other computing and communications technologies (CSTB, 1994a).

By providing access (often over the Internet) to state-of-the-art computer resources and to expertise to help researchers learn how to use them, the HPCCI has also enabled research in a wide range of science and engineering disciplines to be performed that would not otherwise have been possible. Appendix D lists relevant examples from the Grand Challenge activities, and Appendix E points out instances related to the NSF supercomputer center activities, which fall under the HPCCI umbrella despite having some separate roots.

Within the NREN program, NSFNET and other components such as ESNet and the NASA Science Internet have helped to extend networking across the science research community (CSTB, 1994d). Through the internetworking provided by the Internet, connectivity and experimentation with network-based infrastructure have begun to spread rapidly beyond the research community into primary and secondary education, government, industry, and other elements of the private sector (CSTB, 1994d). The Internet has demonstrated the value of widespread access to a common, sophisticated, and increasingly integrated technology base, and it illustrates how a small investment by the federal government can be highly leveraged by additional investments from industry.[24]

The HPCCI approach to developing high-performance computing and communications infrastructure has been affirmed in similar steps taken recently by the Japanese government and industry. David Kahaner of the Office of Naval Research has chronicled Fujitsu's progress in developing parallel processing technology, noting its establishment of research facilities providing worldwide access to its systems in order to obtain the large user base needed to refine its hardware designs and, in particular, to develop the software and applications required to make systems successful (Kahaner, 1994a). Kahaner has also reported on Japanese plans and progress for upgrading high-performance capabilities in public institutions, noting, among other things, the Japanese government's increasing emphasis on basic research.[25]

Increasing Researcher-Developer-User Synergy

The HPCCI has fostered productive interactions among the researchers and developers involved in creating high-performance computing and communications technology and those who use this technology in their own work, most notably computational scientists, but also a broad spectrum of other users. Building on the varying needs and perspectives of the three groups, complex problems are being solved in unique ways.

In particular, the HPCCI has funded cross-disciplinary teams associated with the Grand Challenge projects to solve complex computational problems and produce new software for the new parallel systems. These teams interact with hardware and operating system/compiler researchers and developers to address complex problems through use of the largest computer systems, including those housed at the NSF supercomputer centers. Their work has provided vendors with key insights into the limitations of their architectures.[26] Although these users' requirements are more specialized than those typical of the commercial market for parallel systems, such collaborative work has contributed to enhancing the development and application of high-performance computing and communications technologies. For example, astrophysicists' work on problems in cosmology has stimulated improved handling of fast Fourier transforms in high-performance system compilers that has also benefited commercial applications of seismology in oil exploration.[27]

Like collaboration in other areas, that between computer and computational scientists has not always come easily. In particular, there has been some controversy concerning the relative emphasis on advancing disciplinary knowledge, on the one hand, and advancing the state of the art in high-performance computing and communications, on the other. Nevertheless, the HPCCI has provided a structure and a set of incentives to foster collaborations that many computational scientists believe would not be supported under programs aimed at nurturing individual disciplines.[28]

Impact of Broad Collaboration

Many notable HPCCI accomplishments are the result of broad collaborations. In many instances, they build on foundations that predated the HPCCI, although HPCCI funding, facilities, and focus may have provided the push needed for their realization. The Mosaic browser (Box 2.1) epitomizes both the cumulative nature and broad impact of the development of technologies associated with the HPCCI.

- The HPCCI has driven progress on Grand Challenge problems in disciplines such as cosmology, molecular biology, chemistry, and materials science. Parallel computation has enhanced the ability to do rapid simulations in science and engineering (Kaufmann and Smarr, 1993). Recognition of this development continues to spread across the research community.

- The HPCCI has furthered the development of new modes of analyzing and/or visualizing complex data and in many cases has contributed to more effective interworking between supercomputers and desktop graphics workstations. Visualizations of the numerical output of the largest computers require specialized graphics computers, whose speed would have made them supercomputers in their own right a few years ago. Examples include visualization of complex motions of large biomolecules, intricate engineering assemblies, and the large-scale structure in the universe.

- The HPCCI has made parallel computing widely accepted as the practical route to achieving high-performance computing, as can be seen in the recent growth in sales of parallel systems.[29] Although the market for larger-scale parallel-processing systems is inherently small, it is nevertheless growing. Box 2.2 gives a few of many possible examples of the applications being developed.

BOX 2.1 Mosaic and the World Wide Web

The development in 1993 of the National Center for Supercomputing Applications (NCSA) Mosaic browser shows how the HPCCI has been able to create successful new applications enabled both by new capabilities and by prior developments in information technology.

The forerunner of the Internet (ARPANET) was developed in the late 1960s to link computers and scientists performing defense-related research throughout the United States. By the time of the HPCCI's formal initiation in FY 1992, the Internet had become the most popular network linking researchers and educators at the post-secondary level throughout the world. The development of gopher at the University of Minnesota in the early 1990s was a key step in establishing the Internet as an information resource that could be used through a consistent user interface. At about the same time, researchers at the European Laboratory for Particle Physics, CERN, had developed and implemented the World Wide Web (WWW), a network-based hypertext system that allowed the linking of one piece of information to another across the network. Users accessed WWW information through "browsers" that allowed them to activate a hypertext link in a document to retrieve and display related information regardless of its physical location. Early browsers were text-based, presenting the user with a menu of numbered choices, whereas slightly later browsers made use of the "point-and-click" capabilities of the mouse within a graphical user interface. The WWW and its browsers sought to present users with a consistent interface with which to access all existing methods of Internet navigation and information retrieval.

Meanwhile, the HPCCI had provided funding for research into advanced networking technologies and for the deployment of a high-capacity backbone, enabling the rapid transfer of large amounts of data across the network. In 1993, software developers at the NCSA, one of the centers supported by HPCCI funds from the National Science Foundation, developed an easy-to-use graphical browser for the WWW known as NCSA Mosaic, or sometimes simply Mosaic. It allowed the inclusion of images in WWW documents and even allowed the images themselves to be links to other information. Continuing development of Mosaic enabled the inclusion of audio and video "clips" within hypermedia documents. By November 1993, Mosaic browsers were available for the three most popular computer operating environments: Apple Macintosh, Microsoft Windows, and X Window on UNIX platforms. One year later, users have downloaded more than 1 million copies of Mosaic software, NCSA's scalable WWW server (the world's busiest) is handling over 4 million connections per week, and Mosaic is credited by many for the current and dramatic surge in use of and interest in the Internet.

Perhaps even more significantly, Mosaic has served as the genesis of a wide range of commercial developments. The University of Illinois, which owns the intellectual property associated with Mosaic, has named Spyglass, Inc. as the master sublicenser for the software. So far over 20 companies have licensed Mosaic, creating over 12 million commercially licensed copies. In addition, other companies such as Netscape, IBM, Pipeline, Booklink, MCC, and NetManage have created alternative WWW browsers.

Many other entities have become information providers (a 100-fold increase in WWW servers has occurred in the last 2 years), and new security additions to the underlying Mosaic/WWW infrastructure have enabled electronic commerce on the Internet. Spectacular growth in commercial use of this new information infrastructure is expected in 1995 and beyond because of the relative ease with which the Mosaic/WWW combination allows for highly accessible information servers to be established on the global network. Because of the decentralized nature of the Internet, it will be difficult to gauge the total business income generated by the introduction of Mosaic; however, there is already enough commercial activity to believe that there will be significant payback on the critical federal HPCCI investment in the NSF supercomputer centers that led to this unexpected software development. Even more important is the paradigm shift in the use of the Internet that Mosaic and the WWW have generated.

BOX 2.2 Solutions to Complex Problems

Parallel computing has enabled creative solutions to a number of industrial and scientific problems. The following examples are but a few of many possible illustrations of such successes.

- *Defense.* Simulation of the interaction between the electromagnetic spectrum and various aircraft design features has enhanced the performance of stealth aircraft. Parallel computing enabled rapid calculations for many different wave lengths and aircraft parts.

- *Petroleum.* Oil exploration and production have been made more productive by three-dimensional analysis and visualization of hugh amounts of seismic data. Parallel computing enabled the move from two- to three-dimensional processes.

- *Finance.* Forecasting and simulation of various trading strategies for mortgage-backed security instruments has created a new market and contributed to a reduction in rate spreads. Parallel computing enables simultaneous calculations for numerous instruments within the very short time frames of a fast-moving market. Growth of the finance market arena will provide market pull that should help lower the costs of high-performance processing systems for all types of users.

- The HPCCI has provided large numbers of academic scientists with peer-reviewed access to their choice of high-performance computing architecture to enable their computational science projects. The NSF supercomputing centers, whose core budgets are entirely within the HPCCI, provided access to 23 high-performance computing machines in FY 1995 to 7,500 academic researchers in over 200 universities. The capacity of the centers' supercomputers was 75 times as great as in FY 1986, their first full year of operation, and users represented a broad range of scientific and engineering disciplines (Appendix E lists representative projects).

- The Internet, the flagship of the NREN component of the HPCCI, has become the basis for computer-mediated communication and collaboration among researchers and others. The geographical dispersion of Grand Challenge team members has resulted in pioneering use of electronic collaboration methods, beginning with conventional electronic mail and expanding to multimedia electronic mail, audio and video conferencing, and shared tools for accessing and using remotely stored data and for controlling remote instruments. Development of these methods and tools has been fostered and funded by the HPCCI, demonstrating the potential for electronic collaborators and other approaches to using information technology to support distributed work (CSTB, 1993, 1994e).

- The Internet plus a collection of advances and applications in data storage, analysis, retrieval, and representation—some involving high-performance technology—has catalyzed exploration of digital library concepts. Early Internet-based collaborations among computer scientists, information scientists, cognitive and social scientists, and domain-specific groups provided the basis for a multidisciplinary research effort in digital libraries under the IITA program that was launched in mid-1993 (NSF, 1993).

- The gigabit network testbeds, an element of the NREN component of the HPCCI, pioneered in advancing the frontiers of communication bandwidth essential to achieving enhancements envisioned for the nation's information infrastructure. In the process, they helped to bridge the gap in perspective and emphasis between the computing and communications research communities.

Transfer of Expertise and Technology

In addition to enabling explicit collaborations, the HPCCI has indirectly affected industry and other sectors outside of academia by stimulating the spread of human experts and thus the transfer of technology, building on a tradition of interaction typical of the computing field. As Kenneth Flamm observed, "People are clearly the medium in which computer technology has been stored and transmitted. The history of the computer industry is the history of trained individuals acquiring knowledge—formal and informal—[and] then applying that knowledge, often in a new organizational or institutional setting" (Flamm, 1988, p. 3).[30] The importance of educated and trained talent is reflected in the HPCCI's Basic Research and Human Resources component, which produces the intellectual and human capital, the most general benefit and therefore perhaps the least easy to identify.

Impact on Mission Agencies

In addition to its broad national accomplishments, the HPCCI's contributions to the federal mission agencies, the initial customers for high-performance computing and communications technology, must also be considered. Based on its discussions with agency officials and its own insights into the fit between these technologies and agency activities, the committee believes that the existing and potential contribution of high-performance computing and communications technology to federal mission agencies does justify the investment. The policy decision to eliminate nuclear weapons testing has greatly increased the need for high-performance computer simulations at the Departments of Energy and Defense, for example, and the need to control costs for defense materiel makes simulation in the manufacture of defense-related products an attractive prospect.[31] Thus much of the HPCCI effort at the Advanced Research Projects Agency (ARPA) relates to design and simulation. Although defense-specific applications are sometimes unique, applications-related investment can have impacts beyond meeting agency needs. As in the case of the gigabit testbeds, for example, such work can provide proofs of concept that encourage private investment by lowering risks.

Five Gigabit Testbed Projects: Collaboration and Impact

The gigabit testbeds provide a case study of how to achieve progress through cross-sectoral, developer-user collaboration to advance high-performance computing and communications technologies. Since 1989, the testbeds have provided the means to test applications and thus extend the state of the art in gigabit networking to link high-performance computers to each other and to applications sites. The five original gigabit testbed projects, funded by NSF and ARPA and administered by the Corporation for National Research Initiatives, were started as a 5-year program.[32] They received considerable support from the telecommunications industry, mainly in the form of donated transmission facilities. All three major long-distance carriers and all of the major local-exchange carriers participated. In addition, at least three similar independent testbeds were created through public-private partnerships in the United States, and imitators sprang up in Europe. The testbeds were intended to address two key questions: (1) How does one build a gigabit network?, and (2) What is the utility of such a network?

All five became operational by 1993, showing that gigabit networks could be built. They were largely but not completely successful in illuminating how best to build a gigabit network.[33] The difficulties in many cases were not with the networks but rather the computers connected by the networks, which could not handle the very high bandwidths. Although no research on computer architecture was included in the testbed projects, the projects demonstrated the need for better computer systems, both hardware and software, to achieve better communications—they demonstrated the intimate linkage between computing and communications systems.

As to the utility of the gigabit testbeds, opinions in the community differ sharply. Demonstrations of the potential utility of gigabit networks in some Grand Challenge applications were achieved, including global climate modeling and radiation treatment planning. What is debated was whether the very high bandwidths actually added much value to the applications. No large-scale use of the testbeds for applications research was really possible because of the rather experimental nature of the networking and limited reach of the networks. Also, this work demonstrated that there were essentially no computers that could take advantage of the high-bandwidth gigabit lines because their internal buses were too slow. Although the gigabit testbeds emphasized speed, discussions within the research community, industry, and the HPCCI agencies have suggested that future testbeds should address architecture, scale, and heterogeneity of systems as well as communications speed.

EVOLUTION OF HPCCI GOALS AND OBJECTIVES

Since early 1994, the policy context for the HPCCI has shifted at least twice, and the change in the Congress heralded by the fall 1994 elections suggests the potential for further change.

Improving the Information Infrastructure

The first shift in policy affecting the HPCCI reflected growing interest in the information infrastructure and thus in the universal, integrated, and automated application of computing and communications technologies to meet a wide variety of user needs. The increasing linkage between the HPCCI and information infrastructure can be seen in the "Blue Books," the principal public documentation of the purpose, scope, participation, budget, achievements, and prospects of the HPCCI.[34] Box A.2 in Appendix A outlines the evolution of HPCCI goals as articulated in the Blue Books. Box A.3 indicates the broadening of focus from science to other kinds of applications and drivers of high-performance computing and communications technologies. As discussed above, PL 102-194 marked the first explicit congressional step toward greater attention to information infrastructure; the Blue Books track concurrent thinking of HPCCI agency officials.

The President's FY 1995 budget request bundled the HPCCI together with other items, notably nonresearch programs intended to broaden access to communications and information infrastructure, into the National Information Infrastructure (NII) initiative.[35] The initiative built on the level of technology generally available in the early 1990s, proofs of concept provided by the NREN program, and industry trends, including growing use of computer-based networking within and between a variety of organizations and the rise of a variety of network-based businesses. Once the policy focus—in the government, the press, and most of the agencies—centered on information infrastructure, high-performance computing seemed to be greatly downplayed. In many 1993 and 1994 government documents and administration speeches, the first "C" of HPCCI effectively disappeared, notwithstanding the fact that achieving many of the goals for improving the information infrastructure would depend on rapid continuation of progress in high-performance computing. The NII, previously absent, was featured in subtitles of the 1994 and 1995 Blue Books even though there is no formal, specific NII research program.

The formulation of the NII initiative raised questions about the nature and extent of political support for the original HPCCI objectives, and it may have led to expectations that were not embodied in the HPCCI as originally proposed. It perhaps inadvertently underscored the misperception that because the HPCCI emphasizes the high end of the technology spectrum, it is less relevant or useful than the NII initiative. Cast in more populist terms, the NII initiative included a variety of efforts to explore broadening access to increasingly sophisticated computing and communications services and attention to associated practical concerns. These perceptions—and misperceptions—threaten to slow the momentum of the HPCCI at just the time when its potential to support improvement of the information infrastructure is most needed.

The missing link appears to be the failure of some HPCCI critics to appreciate the dynamism of computing and communications technology: almost by definition, relatively few really need and/or can afford leading-edge computing and communications. But as demonstrated in Chapter 1, the rapid pace of technical development quickly brings these technologies into the mainstream, and they become accessible to a broad populace. Attention to performance is justified by the expectation for rapid transitions from leading-edge technologies to cost-effective, ubiquitous technologies—as well as the kinds of applications expected to grow. For example, multimedia communications will require high-bandwidth, low-delay delivery based on high peak network capacity and on protocol support for negotiating and enforcing service guarantees. The Internet and efforts associated with the development of digital libraries already illustrate the importance of high-performance computing and communications to a broad set of information infrastructure capabilities.

Greater attention to information infrastructure does not imply that performance should be abandoned. But rather than drive toward a narrow goal, such as a teraflop machine or gigabit network, per se, the goal should be systems that scale over several orders of magnitude. This goal should include not only processing rates and communication rates, but also storage capacity, data transfer rates, and retrieval times, as well as the problems inherent in serving millions of users.

One can view information technology as a tent: the height of the center pole corresponds to speed and the breadth of the base corresponds to scale (Figure 2.1). Both speed and scale are important research issues. The HPCCI's focus has been mainly, though not exclusively, on speed. We can move toward an enhanced national information infrastructure by adding more cloth to the tent so as to further emphasize scale without deemphasizing speed, or by shifting the focus somewhat from height to breadth, from the research issues of speed to those of scale. Both changes are appropriate; both dimensions are important for the tent to work. Additional opportunities and needs are also suggested by the tent metaphor, recognizing that there is more to advancing information technology and the information infrastructure than speed and scale. Other important goals include:

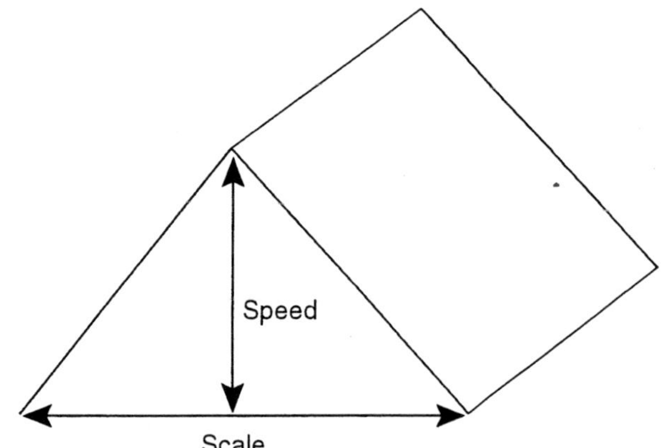

FIGURE 2.1 Scale and speed—important dimensions of the information technology "tent."

- Reliability (Will the tent stay up?);
- Software productivity (How long to move the tent to a new site?);
- Malleability (Can the tent's shape be changed?);
- Human-computer interface (Can people use the tent?); and
- Intelligent search and retrieval (Can people find what they want in the tent?).

Advancing the information infrastructure presents many practical and some urgent needs, but it has been and can continue to be a driver for the long-term research challenges addressed by the HPCCI. High-performance computing and communications will help provide the technologies needed to provide flexible, high-rate, affordable data communications. In Office of Management and Budget guidance for developing FY 1996 R&D budgets, the HPCCI is acknowledged as "helping develop the technological foundation upon which the NII will be built," as a prelude to the articulation of several priorities under the broad goal of "harnessing information technology," one of six broad goals.[36] See Box 2.3 for an illustrative discussion of how telemedicine needs, for example, can help to drive high-performance computing and communications technology development and deployment, and how the HPCCI can foster paradigm shifts in application domains.

Evolving Research Directions and Relevance for the Information Infrastructure

The public debate over information infrastructure is at heart a debate over how to make computing and communications systems easier to use, more effective, and more productive. The challenge for research policy is to translate usability needs into research topics and programs. The HPCCI itself was built on the recognition that the fundamental challenge to greater acceptance and use of high-performance technologies is to make them more usable. Since the 1970s it has been recognized that more usable parallel processing machines imply the development of algorithms, programming support software, and native parallel applications, but the problem persists despite considerable progress. (See Appendix A.) For information infrastructure in the fullest sense—reaching to ordinary citizens—these efforts must be extended to address intuitive models of use and supporting user interface technologies to enable a class of information appliances that will become a part of everyday life. The acceptance and popularity of Mosaic demonstrate the importance of user models, human factors, and other areas where research is critically needed.

More generally, intelligent information retrieval systems, systems for understanding speech and pictures, and systems for enabling intelligent dialogues between people and computer systems are capabilities that will build on HPCCI research and enhance the usefulness and level of use of information infrastructure. In addition, research and development of core software technologies are needed to achieve progress in security, privacy, network measurement and management, transaction processing, application integration, and other capabilities that may be less directly visible to individuals but that make computing and communications facilities more usable. For example, HPCCI and other computing and communications research can enhance capabilities for distributed, remote measurements of quantities that relate to the environment, traffic flows and management, or health conditions. Yet other research should build on the movement to digital transmission of more and more information. As this list of possibilities suggests, information infrastructure is bigger than an initiative, although one or more initiatives, including the HPCCI, can help to organize and accelerate progress in developing and using it.

Complicating decision making regarding information infrastructure research is the recognition that an advanced information infrastructure is not something that will spring full-grown from any one development. Rather, it is something that will grow from new capabilities in many different sectors of the economy and society. Having to provide for migration, evolution, integration, and interoperability compounds the technical challenges.

BOX 2.3 Telemedicine: An Example of HPCCI-Enabled Tele-expertise

The provision of expert professional services, such as medicine, law, and education, is a current consumer of HPCC technologies as well as a driver of future developments. Generically, this provision of services is often referred to as tele-expertise and can be thought of as the live, interactive provision of services and education between individuals who are geographically separated but electronically connected. Tele-expertise holds the promise of reducing costs and lessening geographical disparity in the availability of services. In particular, telemedicine will be an important part of the National Challenge in health care as evidenced by funding from the National Institutes of Health and other organizations for several projects, including a 3-year contract to use advanced network technologies to deliver health services in West Virginia.

Functionally, telemedicine supplies an audio, visual, and data link designed to maximize understanding between provider and patient. In telemedicine, visual contact and scrutiny are particularly important to accurate communication: studies have suggested that body language and facial expression can convey up to 80 percent of meaning. Clinically, although touch is currently denied, video zoom capability often augments visual examinations beyond what is the norm in face-to-face services. In addition, various endoscopes and physiometers may be utilized across a network to further enhance a health care worker's observations.

Limited telemedicine field trials began in 1958 and expanded with federally funded research demonstrations between 1971 and 1980. Considerable research was done on reliability, diagnostic replicability, user satisfaction, and multiple-specialty services. Currently, a few projects address tele-expertise more broadly by combining telemedicine and distance learning, and trials are being conducted in Montana and Texas that encourage the integrated use of remote services in medicine, industry, law, and education, the "MILES" concept. More specifically, telemedicine has made some advances in the years since the early trials:

- Elaboration and extension of transmission media from early microwave and satellite channels to 384-Kbps service and direct fiber-optic links;
- Reduction of costs due to digital signal compression and decreased long-distance rates in constant dollars; and
- Expansion of the number of pieces of medical equipment that may be connected to the remote terminal, chiefly a variety of endoscopes and physiometers.

Nonetheless because of health care cost issues and large disparities in the medical services available in different geographical areas, telemedicine has great potential impact as a National Challenge application for HPCCI technologies. Telemedicine urgently needs several HPCCI-related technologies that can be deployed rapidly and inexpensively and that scale well. Among others, these include:

- *Rapid, high-capacity, multipoint switching.* The telephone became increasingly useful as improved switching and networks enabled rapid expansion across the nation. So it is with interactive video—improved switching and networks will activate the distance-spanning benefits of the interactive video market.

- *Translators to interconnect divergent computing and communications technologies.* New technologies are being developed and deployed so rapidly and in so many different places on the globe that it may be more feasible to develop facile, high-performance translators than to struggle for standards.
- *Compact video storage and good retrieval techniques.* Transparent technologies must be developed to enable a physician to efficiently store and easily retrieve salient clinical moments without distracting from the clinical challenge at hand.

SOURCE: Committee on Information and Communication (1994), p. 28.

Although the U.S. telecommunications industry is a world leader in developing and deploying networks on a large scale, the concepts inherent in an advanced national information infrastructure go beyond connecting a large number of relatively homogeneous end systems supporting a relatively small number of applications, such as today's telephones or televisions. Learning how to build large-scale systems, like learning how to build high-performance ones, requires research; it is not simply a matter of deploying lots of boxes and wires. Envisioned for an advanced national information infrastructure is the interconnection of a much larger number and variety of networks than are interconnected today, with more nodes and switches per network and new mixes of wireline and wireless transmission. The end systems of such networks will run a much wider set of applications and call for a broader set of software-based support capabilities often referred to as "middleware." There will be great complexity, increasing the emphasis on scale and architecture and on areas such as accommodating heterogeneity of systems, decentralization of control and management, routing, security, information navigation and filtering, and so on, all of which will depend on software.

The evolutionary nature of information infrastructure also underscores the importance of engaging industry in the planning, support, and conduct of research. Advisory committees and collaborative projects are but two examples of how this engagement can be achieved. See Appendix B, Box B.1, for a discussion of the development of asynchronous transfer mode as an illustration of fruitful industry-university-government interaction.

There have been many government, academic, and industry efforts, some still under way, to identify and clarify research issues associated with improving information infrastructure. The recent CSTB report *Realizing the Information Future* (1994d) provides a unifying conceptual framework from which it derives strategic emphases for research; a multiparty effort generated several lists of research ideas (Vernon et al., 1994); a more focused workshop generated ideas for funding under the NSF networking and communications research program (NSF, 1994); and ARPA's NETS program and other programs have continued to develop and enrich a technology base for bitways and mid-level services to support defense-relevant applications.[37]

Common to these various efforts is the need for research to enhance such critical information infrastructure middleware capabilities as security and reliability; the basic research underlying many of these concepts had been done by high-performance computing and communications researchers funded mainly by ARPA. In addition, it is important to advance true communications research, including such fundamental areas as transmission, switching, coding and channel access protocols realized in electronic, optical, and wireless technologies, as well as basic computer networking research in such areas as internetworking protocols, transport protocols, flow and congestion control, and so on. These complement and enable efforts relating to distributed computing, which tends to be concerned with the upper or applications level of a total system. See Box 2.4 in the section "Coordination Versus Management" below and Appendix B for an examination of HPCCI communications research efforts and Appendix C for the larger budget allocation picture. Now is the time to explore a wide variety of technical problems, enlisting as many approaches and perspectives as possible.

Overall Computing and Communications R&D Planning

The second major influence on the policy context for HPCCI is a broad rethinking of computing and communications R&D, building on the reorganization of the federal coordinating structures for R&D and factoring in a broad range of technology and policy objectives. The broadest coordination of computing and communications research and development activities across federal agencies is the responsibility of the Committee on Information and Communications (CIC) under the National Science and Technology Council. The CIC was formed in 1994 and is led by the director of defense research and engineering, the associate director for technology of OSTP, and the assistant director of Computer and Information Science and Engineering, NSF. In late-1994, the CIC launched a strategic planning activity to provide input into the FY 1996 budget-setting process, expected to conclude in early 1995, and inform efforts for the next 5 years. Indications from briefings based on preliminary versions of that strategic plan show a broader and richer set of concerns than previously evident.

Strategic focus areas identified in preliminary materials include global-scale information infrastructure technologies, scalable systems technologies, high-confidence systems, virtual environments, user-centered interfaces and tools, and human resources and education. The HPCCI relates at least somewhat to all of these topics, and the planning process is examining where other, mission-related agency activities can build on HPCCI as well as other activities. Key research activities are classified as components, communications, computing systems, software toolkits, intelligent systems, information management, and applications.[38] Software and usability are cross-cutting themes.

Toward a Better Balance

There is a natural evolution of the HPCCI, many aspects of which are associated with improvement of the information infrastructure. The newest component of the HPCCI, the Information Infrastructure Technology and Applications (IITA) program, is one of the most visible signs of this evolution, but also important are the trends within the programs at both ARPA and NSF, which show increasing emphasis on software solutions and tools. ARPA, for example, is devoting attention to software and tools to support design and simulation for development of defense systems; its emphases on security and scalable systems both involve substantial effort relating to software.[39] This evolution should continue and indeed accelerate.

Practical experience with the HPCCI and the volatile policy context both suggest that the ideal research agenda for high-performance computing and communications should be driven by strategic priorities, but focused more broadly than on just those priorities. A stable yet flexible approach would combine substantial focus on goals of current national importance, including directly targeted research, with a flexible program that sustains a healthy base of computing, computation, and communications science and technology. The comprehensiveness of the emerging CIC strategic plan appears to provide a broader platform than previously available for supporting the nation's public computing and communications R&D, including that relating to high-performance technology. Also, the commendable inclusion of a technology "maturity model" in CIC's preliminary strategic planning material illustrates recognition of the technology "trickle-down" phenomenon.

MOVING FORWARD—BASIC ISSUES

Balance of Private and Public Investment

The possibility of reduction or even premature termination of the HPCCI, suggested by congressional requests for inquiries by the General Accounting Office (GAO) and the Congressional Budget Office (CBO) and for this committee's report, is troubling. (See Appendix A for a brief discussion of issues raised by GAO and CBO.)[40] Some HPCCI critics expect industry to pick up the task. They seem to assume possible a larger program of basic research from industry than is reasonable based on history, the growth in competition, which reduces the profit margins needed to sustain R&D, and the economics of innovation generally.

Leading-edge high-performance computing and communications technology is aimed at the most demanding customers, a niche or subset on the order of 10 percent of the larger computing and communications market. Truly high-end systems tend to be nonstandard and to require considerable customer support, for example, which limits their market potential. It may be more appropriate, therefore, to assume that truly high-end systems are aimed at particular classes of problem for which the systems and associated software have particular value, rather than to assume that these systems will become universal. For example, better weather prediction would save an enormous amount of money and should be carried out on high-performance computers even if millions of people do not have them. The lower end of the market will grow as parallel processing vendors reposition their products, addressing broader industrial and commercial needs for information storage and analysis, multimedia servers, data mining, and intelligent transactions systems.[41]

Observers within the computing and communications research communities, including members of this committee, are concerned about the impact of computer and communications industrial restructuring. Changes in the organization of these industries, plus the inherent difficulties incumbent companies face in using research results, prevent companies from undertaking the kind of large-scale, long-range research needed to tackle the challenges inherent in advancing the HPCCI objectives or the broader objectives associated with information infrastructure. This concern is almost impossible to substantiate, because it is inherently intuitive, albeit shaped by expert judgment and the experience of committee members working in or with a variety of computing and communications companies, and because the results of current trends will not be evident for several years.[42]

Coordination Versus Management

The HPCCI became an integrated, multiagency, cross-cutting initiative because agency and congressional officials recognized that there would be economies of scale and scope from connecting complementary efforts across research disciplines and funding agencies.[43] By cooperating, agency officials have successfully leveraged the dollars available in the initiative budget, facilitating collaborative efforts with industry. The NREN infrastructure investments, including the NSFNET backbone and gigabit testbeds, provide examples. Network connections, research tools, and delivery of educational products appear to motivate the broadest interagency activity within the HPCCI context, helping to extend collaborations beyond the conduct of research per se and into a wider circle of agencies.

Through its accomplishments and esprit de corps, the HPCCI has become a model for multiagency collaboration.[44] Each agency retains responsibility for its own part of the program, focusing its participation to meet agency needs and resources. The voluntary compliance of HPCCI agencies with the spirit of PL 102-194 reflects the special cooperation that has characterized the HPCCI. These conditions have enabled the initiative to grow and adapt relatively quickly to changing national needs, technology prospects, and the fit between the two. Perhaps because they see themselves as principal architects of the program, officials from the four initial HPCCI agencies (Department of Defense (DOD), Department of Energy (DOE), National Aeronautics and Space Administration (NASA), and National Science Foundation), in particular, have carried high levels of enthusiasm, dedication, inventiveness, and energy into undertaking the HPCCI. These intangible qualities are widely recognized within the computing and communications research community.

The level of interagency coordination observed today took time to grow. As one might expect when organizations with different missions, budgets, and cultures are faced with a joint task, the HPCCI agencies have disagreed on issues of emphasis and approach over the years. For example, DOE and NSF have had different views on evolving the NREN program with respect to scope and speed. What is important for the future of the HPCCI, however, is not that differences have arisen but rather that legitimate differences owing to varying missions have been respected, and cooperation and coordination have improved over time. For example, NSF and ARPA—which respectively emphasize small science and larger projects—have worked well in the management of their joint network and computing research activities, as described in Box 2.4.

BOX 2.4 Coordination in Practice:
The Case of Communications R&D

The HPCCI currently includes a relatively modest but vigorous communications research program. Three large programs account for $77 million of the HPCCI communications research budget. Research is concentrated mainly in four areas (see Appendix B for more details and context):

1. Optical networks (the longest-term research),
2. Gigabit networking (medium-term research),
3. Multimedia communications (fairly near term research), and
4. Internetwork scaling (near- and medium-term applied research).

The ARPA networking program, at $43.1 million, is the largest communications research program activity. The milestones include:

- Demonstration of diverse Internet capabilities such as cable and wireless bitways,
- Demonstration of rate-adaptive quality of service negotiation in asymmetric networks,
- Demonstration of bandwidth and service reservation guarantees for networks in support of real-time services,
- Demonstration of secure routing systems, and
- Interconnection of gigabit testbeds.

The ARPA Global Grid program, at $23 million, intends to accomplish (in 1995):

- Demonstration of multi-wavelength reconfigurable optical network architecture, and
- Demonstration of integrated DOD and commercial networks in support of crisis management applications.

NSF's Very High Speed Networks and Optical Systems program, at $11 million, supports research in a wide variety of high-performance networking technologies, including:

- Gigabit testbed research (switching, protocols, and management);
- Resource discovery;
- Information theory;
- Network security;
- Modulation, detection, and coding for information storage; and
- Optical networking.

ARPA and NSF have coordinated well to avoid duplication of efforts. ARPA funds most of the research on internetworking, and NSF concentrates on the deployment of internetworking infrastructure via its NSFNET activities. NSF and ARPA have jointly funded the gigabit testbed research program, which involves demonstration of cross-country gigabit networking technologies.

With the reinforcement provided by PL 102-194, the set of agencies involved in the HPCCI grew. This broader participation better positions the HPCCI to support development and application of computing and communications technologies essential to improving the nation's information infrastructure. However, as reflected in both executive and congressional efforts to promote such improvements, the information infrastructure raises issues such as deployment, regulation, and other practical aspects that require engaging a broader and somewhat different set of agencies, such as the Federal Communications Commission, the National Telecommunications and Information Administration, and so on, to address a wider range of issues than those relating to R&D.

The diversity of the HPCCI approach allows many views to compete, first for funding, later in the evolution of thinking among researchers, and finally in the marketplace. It also fosters pursuit of the intellectual questions posed by the HPCCI via a range of complementary modes including classical single principal-investigator (PI) research, multiple-PI experimental research, multiple-PI/multiple-field collaborations, intramural research in institutes and national laboratories, and joint industry-government-academia experiments or proofs of concept.

A variety of mechanisms are used to foster interagency cooperation and coordination:

- Joint funding of projects, from relatively specific or narrow activities to the federal portions of the Internet;
- Consortia, such as the consortium on Advanced Modeling of Regional Air Quality involving six federal agencies plus several state and local governments;
- The MetaCenter concept pursued by NSF supercomputer centers (see Appendix E) and extending to other entities and users via the MetaCenter Regional Affiliates program; and
- Cross-agency reviews of grants and contracts, such as the NSF, ARPA, and NASA digital library initiative, and joint testbeds.

The diversity in approach and tactics makes it less likely that the nation will miss some important approach. It also facilitates participation by a variety of agencies, which tend to have different styles as well as emphases for supporting research or procuring technology, consistent with their different missions, histories, and cultures.

As to diversity of mechanisms, the multiple-PI/multiple field category is epitomized by the Grand Challenge teams, which involve multiple institutions attacking frontier research problems with multiple-year horizons, often drawing on access to the leading-edge machines in the NSF supercomputer centers and benefiting from interactions between computer scientists and computational scientists.[45] The joint industry-government-academia experiment category is currently epitomized by the gigabit network testbeds. More specifically, NASA's FY 1995 HPCCI effort includes integrated multidisciplinary computational aerospace vehicle design and multidisciplinary modeling and analysis of earth and space science phenomena (Holcomb, 1994).

Coordinating Structure

The coordinating structure of the HPCCI has evolved steadily, largely in response to external pressures for improved visibility of decision making, requirements for accountability for expenditures, and the flow of information into and out of the initiative. Some HPCCI observers have continued to argue for a more uniform approach to related activities with thorough planning, precise milestones, and presumably no wasted effort, in a more centralized program. This is the essence of early criticism lodged by the Computer Systems Policy Project (1991 and 1993).

Drawbacks of Centralization

The central question about coordination is whether the special vitality of HPCCI would survive and whether centralized control would convey sufficient benefits, or merely disrupt current arrangements. A more centralized approach would have several drawbacks that could vitiate the

HPCCI: potential loss of variety in perspectives on applications now arising from agencies with different missions; greater risk of concentrating on the wrong thing; and increased bureaucratic overhead and costs associated with efforts to overlay separate programs. Moreover, because much of the existing effort involves previously existing programs, there is a risk that agencies would not participate in a program that involved a loss of their control to a more centralized authority. This concern, probably paramount to the agencies, arises from the recognition that much of the funding associated with the HPCCI is not new, just classified as relevant to the initiative. A virtue of the current arrangement is that the central coordination is provided by a relatively small entity that lacks the resources for micromanagement. That approach maximizes the benefits provided by a diverse group of agencies.

National Coordination Office

BOX 2.5 National Coordination Office:
Staffing and Structure through 1994

Chaired by the director of the National Coordination Office (NCO), the High Performance Computing, Communications, and Information Technology (HPCCIT) Subcommittee and its Executive Committee coordinate planning, budgeting, implementation, and program review for the overall initiative. The HPCCIT Subcommittee has also been the major vehicle for communication with other federal agencies, the U.S. Congress, and numerous representatives from the private sector.

The director of the NCO reports to the director of the Office of Science and Technology Policy (OSTP). The director of OSTP has specified that overall budget oversight for the HPCCI be provided by the National Science and Technoloy Council through the Committee on Information and Communication (CIC). Actual appropriations for the initiative are made in the regular appropriation bills for each participating agency. The HPCCIT coordinates program and budget planning for the initiative and reports to the CIC.

Under the umbrella of the HPCCIT, several working groups have been formed to help guide and coordinate activities within the five components of the initiative. For example, the Information Infrastructure Technology and Applications Task Group, established in 1993, has encouraged and coordinated participating agencies' plans for research and development aimed at providing needed technologies and capabilities for an enhanced nationwide information infrastructure and the National Challenge applications. The Science and Engineering Computing Working Group coordinates activities and software development relating to Grand Challenge applications.

The direct operating expenses of the NCO are jointly borne by the participating agencies in proportion to their HPCCI budgets, and further support is provided by the interagency detailing of staff to the NCO for varying periods of time. Currently the NCO has eight permanent staff and two staff "on loan" from the Department of Energy. In addition to providing general administrative functions such as payroll and personnel administration, the National Library of Medicine also contributes specialized assistance such as public information functions, budget preparation, legislative analysis and tracking, graphic arts services, procurement, and computing and communications support.

SOURCES: See Lindberg (1994); NCO (1994); and CIC (1994). Additional information from letter dated August 8, 1994, to Marjory Blumenthal (CSTB) from Donald A.B. Lindberg (NCO/NLM) in response to committee's interim report (CSTB, 1994c).

The HPCCI coordination focus lies in the National Coordination Office for High-Performance Computing and Communications, which was established in September 1992. It operates under the aegis of the Office of Science and Technology Policy and the National Science and Technology Council (NSTC; see Figure 2.2). Box 2.5 provides information on the structure and staffing of the NCO.

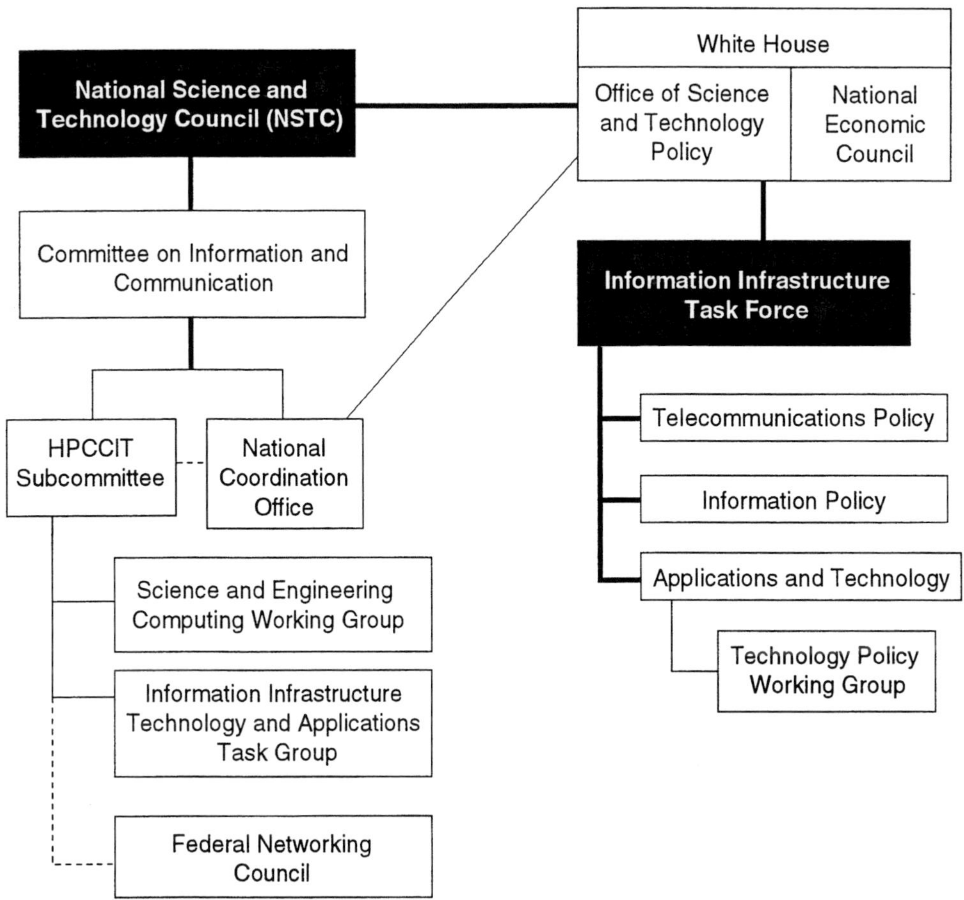

FIGURE 2.2 Organizational context for HPCCI coordination.

The NCO was established to aid interagency cooperation and to serve as liaison for the initiative to the Congress, other levels of government, universities, industry, and the public. It assists the mission agencies in coordinating their separate programs, offering a forum through which the separate agencies can learn of each other's needs, plans, and actions. As part of its coordinating function, the NCO gathers information about the HPCCI activities of different agencies and helps to make this information available to Congress, industry, and the public. Since its formation, the NCO has produced the impressive FY 1994 and FY 1995 Blue Books as visible manifestations of its coordination efforts. The FY 1995 Blue Book is the best documentation available of HPCCI activities and where the money is invested.

Strengthening the NCO. The public debate over the HPCCI attests to the need for improved communication regarding the initiative's purpose and accomplishments. Because lack of external understanding is damaging—not least because it leads to criticisms and investigations that divert energy and resources from pursuing HPCCI goals—the committee believes that the HPCCI could benefit from a stronger NCO that can do a better job of telling the program's many constituencies about its goals and successes; see the committee's Interim Report (CSTB, 1994c) and Chapter 3.

As authorized in the 1991 High Performance Computing Act, the NCO was to have been assisted by an advisory committee that could provide regular infusions of ideas from industry and academia. To date, the HPCCI has been led mostly by computing visionaries and by people active in science and science applications. That is the right kind of leadership to drive the creation of enabling technology and to create computer architectures that are appropriate for the pursuit of science objectives. But the initiative now also needs the perspective on applications and on making computing and communications technologies more usable that would be provided by an advisory committee of recognized experts with membership balanced between academia and industry, and balanced with respect to application areas and the core technologies underlying the HPCCI.[46] The growing dependence of more and more people on infrastructure, the rise in potential liabilities of varying kinds, and growth in competitive challenges from abroad increase industry's stakes in the quality of information technology available. Industry input into such issues as standards, security, reliability, and accounting, for example, becomes more important as advancing the information infrastructure and "high-confidence systems" come to drive more of the research agenda.

In lieu of having an advisory committee, the NCO has taken the initiative to convene some industry and other groups to obtain focused input on HPCCI-related issues and directions. In conjunction with its regular meetings with federal HPCCI agency representatives, the NCO has engaged in dialogues with representatives of the computer systems, software, and telecommunications industries; managers of academic computing centers; and others; and it has held a similar discussion with representatives of the mass information storage industry. It has also participated in workshops, conferences, and public meetings sponsored by participating agencies and the subcommittee on High Performance Computing, Communications, and Information Technology (HPCCIT). However, NCO leadership notes that given the restrictions on external interactions imposed by the Federal Advisory Committee Act, the absence of an official advisory committee prevents it from obtaining needed input on an ongoing basis, limiting it instead to one-time interactions and thus foregoing the insights that can arise where parties benefit from repeated interactions.

The committee echoed the NCO's concern by recommending in its interim report that the long-awaited HPCCI advisory committee be established immediately. In view of the delays and difficulties in establishing an HPCCI advisory committee and the apparent tendency of federal science policy leaders to enfold HPCCI in a larger NII initiative, there is some expectation that one advisory committee may be empaneled to provide input into the broader CIC agenda, and to the HPCCI. This National Research Council committee thinks that solution might work, but it urges some action now.

Understanding the Changing Management Context. Actions taken to reinforce the NCO must account for the larger, evolving administrative and management context in which the NCO fits. A key component of that context is the CIC. It receives limited staff support from OSTP and, presumably, from agency-based staff members. Its members include directors of computer- and communications-related research units from across the federal government. Their participation in the CIC provides information exchange and coordination, but the CIC is not an implementation entity. The NCO director participates in both CIC and HPPCIT.

Planning, coordination, and management for the HPCCI have been further confounded by the rise of additional bodies to address technology policy and other policy relating to the NII initiative. The Information Infrastructure Task Force (IITF), formed in 1993, has a Technology Policy Working Group with overlapping representation with the HPCCIT. Its focus is supposed to be technology policy, versus the HPCCIT's focus on research and development. The IITF receives input from the NII Advisory Committee, also formed in 1993. And on networking issues there are yet more special coordination and advisory entities, such as the Federal Networking Council (FNC) that has associated with it the FNC Advisory Committee. This proliferation of cross-agency entities itself presents many possibilities for confusion. Moreover, by all accounts—from virtually every HPCCI official the committee has heard from and from several private-sector parties—the processes of communication and decision making have been slowed by a calendar-filling profusion of meetings. This situation raises basic practical questions of what work can get done, when, how, and by whom, when committee meetings appear to be the order of the day.

Budget

A detailed overview of the HPCCI budget is presented in Appendix C. The overall level has been subject to misunderstanding.

According to the Blue Books, the HPCCI budget has grown from $489.4 million in FY 1992 to the $1.1 billion requested for FY 1995. When the HPCCI was proposed in the executive budget for FY 1992, the agencies involved identified from their existing FY 1991 activities a base that contributed to the goals of the program. The HPCCI's multiagency budget is more complex than it would be had the program been started "from scratch" within a single agency. Although complexity is inherent in multiagency programs and budgets, it has added to the confusion about spending priorities and accomplishments for the initiative.

The agencies that had activities included in the FY 1992 base were the (Defense) ARPA, DOE, NASA, NSF, National Institute of Standards and Technology, National Oceanic and Atmospheric Administration (NOAA), Environmental Protection Agency, and National Institutes of Health/National Library of Medicine. In each subsequent year, agencies have added to this base in two ways: (1) by identifying additional existing programs that contribute to HPCCI goals and (2) by reprogramming and relabeling agency funds to support relevant aspects of the HPCCI. To this base of "identified" activities, Congress has added some funding each year for new activities or the expansion of existing efforts.

The result is that the $1.1 billion requested for FY 1995 is composed of three elements: (1) funds for the continuation of agency activities that were in existence when the HPCCI started and were designated in the FY 1992 base budget, (2) funds for existing or redirected programs that have since been designated as being a part of the HPCCI, and (3) additional funds for new activities or expansion of existing efforts. It is difficult to determine exactly how large each element is and to make interagency comparisons, because each agency has used slightly different approaches for identifying existing efforts and somewhat different formats for supporting program and budgetary detail. Also, this situation has allowed some agencies (e.g., NOAA) to be considered participants in the initiative without receiving any new money.[47]

NOTES

1. The substance of these components is outlined in the HPCCI's annual Blue Books; see FCCSET (1991, 1993, and 1994).

2. Note that many of the concerns raised here were expressed or articulated in a CSTB report released at the dawn of the HPCCI, *The National Challenge in Computer Science and Technology* (CSTB, 1988).

3. A teraflop refers to 10^{12} (or 1 trillion) floating point operations per second (FLOPS), 1,000 times the performance of the best machines available when the HPCCI began.

4. See Flamm (1988); this book discusses the major computer development projects of the 1940s, 1950s, and 1960s and their dependence on government stimulus and combined government, university, and industry development of technology.

5. In turn, the use of multiple microprocessors in large-scale parallel machines also exposed problems that would have to be resolved for microprocessors as the dominant computing element.

6. See Zatner (1994), pp. 21-25, for a discussion of events leading to Chapter 11 status for TMC. KSR suffered from an accounting scandal, then had to contend with 12 class-action shareholder lawsuits (Snell, 1994). The impact of the lack of software has also been implicated as an indicator of management ineffectiveness in the fates of TMC and KSR (Lewis, 1994).

7. Indeed, talk of the next hurdle, the petaflop system, has already begun. NSF, NASA, DOE, and DOD hosted a 1994 workshop on enabling technologies for petaflop computing. The report is said to argue that that goal can be met at reasonable cost in 20 years using today's paradigms. See Anthes (1994), p. 121.

8. "Recommendation A-2: At the apex of the HPC pyramid is a need for a national capability at the highest level of computing power the industry can support with both efficient software and hardware.

"A reasonable goal for the next 2-3 years would be the design, development, and realization of a national teraflop-class capability, subject to the effective implementation of Recommendation B-1 and the development of effective software and computational tools for such a large machine. Such a capability would provide a significant stimulus to commercial development of a prototype high-end commercial HPC system of the future." (NSF, 1993, p. 11)

9. The fundamental computer unit is the microprocessor, which today has a peak speed of around 300 megaflops. It seems premature to build a 3,000 processor teraflop machine in 1995, but as the microprocessors increase in speed to 1 to 2 gigaflops by the late 1990s, it seems reasonable that 512- to 1024-processor teraflop machines may be built if the economics of users and their applications require it. For example, Kenneth Kliewer, director of the Center for Computational Sciences at Oak Ridge National Laboratory, was quoted in December 1994 as saying: "The scale here is clearly a function of time, but we could have nearly a teraflop computer today by coupling the Oak Ridge and Los Alamos computers with the ones from Cornell and Maui" (Rowell, 1994). In November 1994, a new product announcement by Japan's NEC indicated that the maximum configuration, with a total of 512 processors, could be rated at a theoretical peak of 1 teraflop (Parker-Smith, 1994b).

The committee notes that if trends at the NSF supercomputer centers continue, the MetaCenter (which pools some of the centers' resources) could achieve an aggregate teraflop in mid-FY 1998 and each center would reach a peak teraflop machine by the end of FY 1999. By contrast, even the aggregate performance would not reach a teraflop until after the year 2000 if acquisition of higher-performance architectures were to revert to pre-HPCCI levels.

10. The HPCCI also triggered considerable debate about what broad availability means—what capabilities, in what locations, accessible by whom and at what cost—anticipating the more recent debates about how universal service in telecommunications should evolve.

11. The gigabit goal, as defined in the NSF-ARPA-CNRI testbeds, was to achieve an end-to-end speed of at least 1 Gbps between two computers on a network. The telephone achievement was to multiplex about 25,000 64-Kbps voice conversations onto a transmission line operating at 1.7 Gbps (late 1980s technology, now more than doubled). The gigabit testbeds have demonstrated end-to-end speeds between two computers of about 500 Mbps, limited by the internal bus speeds of the computers, not the network.

12. Comments by Sandy MacDonald, NOAA, at "Environmental Simulation: The Teraflop and Information Superhighway Imperative Workshop," August 18-20, 1994, Monterey, Calif. He noted an increase from 3,200 numerical observations per day for Kansas in 1985 to 86,000 daily observations, many from automated instruments.

13. Comments by Steve Hammond, National Center for Atmospheric Research, at "Environmental Simulation: The Teraflop and Information Superhighway Imperative Workshop," August 18-20, 1994, Monterey, Calif. He observed that teraflop computing helped reduce processing times to 90 seconds per modeled month, yielding 1,000 modeled months in 30 hours of processing time.

14. Briefings to the committee. Legislative codification and appropriation for a broader vision for the HPCCI have been attempted but have been unsuccessful, most recently in connection with S4/H1757, in 1994.

15. For example, in addressing networking, PL 102-194 also anticipated many of the practical concerns associated with enhancements and expansion of the nation's information infrastructure, such as user charging and protection of intellectual property rights.

16. Policy documents emerging from the administration in mid-1994 and congressional actions in 1993-1994 emphasize a commitment to linking R&D spending to strategic, national concerns (Panetta, 1994; NSTC, 1994b).

17. Of course, there will also be people using the technology who are not in close contact with developers and vice versa—hence the value of a solid base of funding for both computing and communications research and for the sciences that increasingly depend on computation.

18. See CSTB (1988) for a discussion of national challenges within computing. See also CSTB (1992) for a discussion of methods of combining intrinsic problems with problems inspired by needs in other areas.

19. The lengthy time scales associated with developing complex computer-based systems are outlined in CSTB (1994a).

20. Rigorous cost-accounting and auditing can be elaborate, costly, and inflexible: "As a result, R&D done under federal contract is inherently more expensive and less effective than R&D done by an organization using its own funds" (Cohen and Noll, 1994, p. 74).

21. The National Coordination Office (NCO) has taken a first step in the evaluation area through its development of the HPCCI implementation plan. The format of the project and program records in that volume provides a basis for subsequent efforts to assess progress. The NCO management has expressed some interest in tracking progress relative to plan elements.

22. The NSF infrastructure program was motivated by the recognition in the late 1970s of major deficiencies in the academic environment for experimental computer science and engineering. The initial stimulus was the report by Feldman and Sutherland (1979). When that report was written, the discipline of computer science and engineering was perceived to be in crisis: faculty members were underpaid relative to research positions in industry and were leaving universities at an increasing rate; the number of new Ph.D.s fell far short of meeting the national demand; most departments lacked experimental computing research facilities; and there was a significant gap in research capability between the top three or four departments, which had benefited from a decade of ARPA investment, and the rest.

23. The Feldman and Sutherland (1979) report resulted in the establishment in 1981 of the Coordinated Experimental Research (CER) program at NSF. The CER program made awards of approximately $1 million per year (including an institutional match of typically 25 percent) for durations of 5 years to support significant experimental research efforts by building the necessary infrastructure. There have been very substantial increases in the number of departments producing strong experimental research, the number of departments producing strong students in experimental areas, the number of departments conducting leading-edge research in a significant number of areas, the overall rate of Ph.D. production in the field, and other similar measures.

The success of the CER program was important in shaping several subsequent NSF programs that also contributed to the infrastructure of the field, such as the Engineering Research Centers (ERCs) program. A number of ERCs are in computing-related areas, which in turn influenced the Science and Technology Centers (STCs) program; three STCs are in computing-related areas. The CER program itself ultimately became the Research Infrastructure program and was complemented by an Educational Infrastructure program. A number of other agencies instituted research and/or educational infrastructure programs.

24. The NSFNET backbone has involved NSF spending authorized on the order of $30 million but complemented by in-kind and other investments by IBM and MCI through Advanced Networks and Services, which has deployed and operated NSFNET under a cooperative agreement with NSF. The Internet overall has been growing through proliferation of a variety of commercial Internet access providers. See CSTB (1994d).

25. "Although the infrastructure, including networking, software applications and tools, visualization capabilities, etc., is still not strong enough, raw computing power is becoming comparable, and in some cases greater than what is available at NSF Centers in the U.S. This increase in resources comes at a time when the Japanese government is also increasing its emphasis on basic research for its own needs and to insure that Japan is viewed as a [sic] equitable contributor to the global science community. Readers might want to reflect on the impact the NSF centers have had on U.S. science output and the potential for this to occur in Japan." (Kahaner, 1994b)

26. For example, as a result of detailed interactions between a high-performance computing and communications vendor and a staff member of an NSF supercomputer center, a Grand Challenge computer code uncovered previously undiscovered hardware bugs in newly released microprocessors installed in a scalable supercomputer at the center. This led to the vendor using a version of the Grand Challenge code inside the company as a standard test to uncover both hardware and compiler bugs.

27. Jeremiah P. Ostriker, Princeton University Observatory, personal communication, December 23, 1994.

28. Jeremiah P. Ostriker, Princeton University Observatory, personal communication, December 23, 1994.

29. Examples include the Silicon Graphics Everest/Challenge systems (some 3500 Challenge, Power Challenge, Onyx, and Power Onyx systems were sold in the 15 months following their September 1993 introduction) and the IBM SP2 and Power Parallel systems; see Parker-Smith, 1994a. See also Appendix A.

30. Even the rise and fall of individual ventures shows this generally positive pattern: TMC was launched in part by the expertise of Danny Hillis, previously at MIT, and his associates. With TMC's contraction in 1994, Hillis' team of over 20 engineers from TMC's Future Systems Group went to Sun Microsystems, where they are working on a scalable massively parallel processing system, while other TMC talent continued with a TMC parallel software descendent (Riggs, 1994).

31. Briefings to committee by Victor Reis (Department of Defense) and Howard Frank (Advanced Research Projects Agency).

32. No follow-on program to the gigabit testbed projects has yet been announced. In July 1994, an NSF and ARPA workshop proposed a research agenda for gigabit networking and called for an experimental gigabit research network facility. NSF and ARPA are extending the existing program by a few months, into early 1995.

33. Note that there is continuing popular confusion over the term "gigabit networks" and the fact that the speed most often quoted for them is 640 megabits per second. Each gigabit connection consists of two one-way circuits, each operating at 640 Mbps. Thus the overall speed of the two-way connection is 1.28 gigabits per second when properly compared to the quoted two-way capacity of application networks. Also, the 640-Mbps circuits in at least one case (Aurora) were derived by splitting 2.4-Gbps trunk circuits.

34. Each year beginning in 1991 the director of the Office of Science and Technology Policy submits a report on the HPCCI to accompany the president's budget. The FY 1992, FY 1993, and FY 1994 books were produced by the now-defunct FCCSET; the FY 1995 report was produced by the NCO (acting for the CIC). The report describes prior accomplishments and the future funding and activities for the coming fiscal year. These reports have collectively become known as "Blue Books" after the color of their cover.

35. The NII initiative was framed in 1993 and included in the FY 1995 budget request.

36. Other goals, such as "a healthy, educated citizenry," also include applications of computing and communications among their priorities.

37. CSTB (1994b); Vernon et al. (1994); and NSF (1994). The ARPA NETS program is covered by the Blue Books for FY 1994 and FY 1995.

38. Briefing to committee by Edward Lazowska, based on a Computing Research Association briefing by John Toole, and augmented by briefings by Anita K. Jones and Howard Frank, December 20, 1994.

39. Briefing to committee by Howard Frank, December 20, 1994.

40. GAO (1993); CBO (1993).

41. Committee briefings by Forest Baskett, Silicon Graphics Inc., April 13, 1994; Justin Ratner, Intel Supercomputer Systems Division, June 27, 1994; Steve Nelson, Cray Research, Inc., June 28, 1994; and Steven Wallach, Convex Computer Corporation, June 28, 1994. Also, see Lewis (1994) re "gigaflops on a budget." See also Furht (1994) for a description of how Encore, Hewlett-Packard, IBM, Pyramid, Tandem, Stratus, and AT&T have changed their focus to transaction processing and fault-tolerant computing.

42. For example, in FY 1994, the NSF centers had an income derived by recovering cycle costs from noncomputer industrial partners of around $1 million to $2 million. In comparison to their NSF Cooperative Agreement level of $16 million per year, this has a small impact. Indeed, the situation is even worse, since a typical NSF supercomputer center receives only half its annual budget from the NSF Cooperation Agreement, the other half coming from state and university matching funds, other grants, and equipment donations by computer vendors.

The center experience also shows that over the last few years, industry spending to attain center know-how—training, software development, information infrastructure application development, virtual reality and visualization projects, and so on—and to use centers as vehicles for collaborative research has increased and exceeds spending on computer processing cycles at some centers. Because the centers have an existing staff for these projects, the industrial income generally covers only the marginal cost of providing that service and therefore does not increase net "new dollars."

43. Other cross-cutting initiatives contemporaneous with HPCCI include advanced manufacturing technology; global change; advanced materials and processing; biotechnology; and science, mathematics, engineering, and technology education (FCCSET, 1993).

44. The HPCCI is understood by a variety of federal officials to have been a model for the "virtual agency" concept advanced through the National Performance Review efforts to improve the organization and effectiveness of the federal government (Gore, 1993).

45. There are 16 grants, 7 awarded in FY 1992 and 9 in FY 1993. Their source of funds can be broken into three parts (NSF/CISE, NSF/non-CISE, and ARPA). The FY 1994 and FY 1995 numbers are shown below. As the chart indicates, CISE's percentage is less than one-third of the funding. This shows great leverage, even greater than that of the centers, roughly one-half of whose budget comes CISE.

	NSF/CISE	NSF/non-CISE	ARPA	TOTAL
FY 1994 $M	2.77	5.00	1.91	9.68
FY 1994 %	29	52	20	100
FY 1995 $M	2.79	4.93	1.44	9.16
FY 1995 %	30	54	16	100

46. For example, NASA feels pressure from the HPCCI objectives to orient its program in certain directions, but is encouraged by the aeronautics industry to orient its activities in other directions. NASA is caught in the middle. Aeronautics industry representation at the HPCCI leadership level could help guide the HPCCI in directions that better support the goal of enhancing U.S. industrial competitiveness.

47. Letter dated August 25, 1994 to Marjory Blumenthal from Jerry D. Mahlman (NOAA) in response to committee's interim report (CSTB, 1994c).

3

Recommendations

The committee believes that strong public support for a broadly based research program in information technology is vital to maintaining U.S. leadership in information technology. Facilitated access for both academic and industrial users to advanced computing and communications technologies has produced further benefits both in scientific progress and in U.S. industrial competitiveness. The committee's recommendations for the High Performance Computing and Communications Initiative (HPCCI) are based on this view of the importance of information technology to the country, as well as on the track record of success for the government's investment in information technology research. The committee's 13 recommendations address five different areas:

- General research program;
- High-performance computing;
- Networking and information infrastructure, including work focusing on the National Challenges;
- The supercomputer centers and the Grand Challenge projects; and
- Coordination and program management.

Within each area the recommendations are presented in priority order.

GENERAL RECOMMENDATIONS

As discussed in Chapter 1, government investment has played a major role in maintaining U.S. leadership in information technology and in helping to advance the technology, providing benefits to virtually every citizen. The return on federal investment has been substantial.

Recommendation 1. Continue to support research in information technology. Ensure that the major funding agencies, especially the National Science Foundation and the Advanced Research Projects Agency, have strong programs for computing research that are independent of any special initiatives. Past investment has yielded significant returns, as demonstrated in Chapter 1. Continued government investment in computing research, *at least as high as the current dollar level,* is critical to continuing the innovation essential to maintaining U.S. leadership.

Today the HPCCI supports nearly all of this research, an arrangement that is both misleading and dangerous: misleading because much important computing research addresses areas other than high performance (even though it may legitimately fit under the new Information Infrastructure Technology and Applications (IITA) component of the HPCCI), and dangerous because reduced funding for the HPCCI could cripple all of computing research. The "war on cancer" did not support all of biomedical research, and neither should the HPCCI or any future initiative on the nation's information infrastructure subsume all of computing research.

Recommendation 2. Continue the HPCCI, maintaining today's increased emphasis on the research challenges posed by the nation's evolving information infrastructure. In addition to the work on infrastructure carried out in the new IITA program, continuing progress is needed in areas addressed by the HPCCI's other four components (High-Performance Computing Systems, National Research and Education Network (NREN), Advanced Software Technology and Algorithms, and Basic Research and Human Resources).

The NSFNET and the gigabit testbeds have demonstrated the ability to build larger-scale, higher-performance networks, but ongoing research in several areas is still needed before a ubiquitous high-performance information infrastructure can be developed and deployed nationwide. The committee supports the HPCCI's increasing focus on information infrastructure, emphasizing that successful evolution of the nation's communications capability rests on continued investment in basic hardware, networking, and software technologies research. To further this evolution, which is consistent with administration efforts, including the addition of the IITA program, plus General Accounting Office (GAO, 1994) and other recommendations, the committee has identified in Recommendations 3 through 10 program areas that should receive (a) increased emphasis, (b) stay at present levels, and (c) have reduced federal support.

RECOMMENDATIONS ON HIGH-PERFORMANCE COMPUTING

Recommendation 3. Continue funding a strong experimental research program in software and algorithms for parallel machines. It is widely recognized that software for parallel computers lags behind hardware development. Progress in software and algorithms for parallel computers will determine how quickly and how easily we can use them.[1] A shift in emphasis toward increased funding for software and algorithm activities under high-performance computing has already begun. This shift properly reflects the urgency of investing more in software.

The committee recommends the following approach to continue progress in research areas critical to developing and building needed software and algorithms:

- Continue research on compilers, programming languages, and tools aimed at making it easier to use parallel computing machines. Critical needs include improved portability across machines, improved ability to run programs on machines of different sizes, and better understanding of how best to use different multiprocessor memory organizations.

- Continue to develop experimental operating systems for parallel computers. More operating system experience will help us learn how to improve parallel hardware. Focus on the underlying research challenges posed by parallel machines rather than developing commercial operating systems technology.

- Continue research on database and information systems for parallel machines. Such applications have increased in importance and represent a promising area for using parallel computing.

- Continue research in the use of parallel computing for graphics and visualization. Graphics applications are valuable both because they demand much from their software and hardware and because they stimulate effective use of high-performance computing by offering computational scientists and other end-users the ability to analyze complex data and problems.

• Fund sufficient hardware purchases to ensure needed access for computer scientists and end users trying to evaluate the effectiveness of new architectures and software technologies. Dedicated access to expensive machines is often required for operating systems development or for controlled measurement of software performance, and sometimes dedicated access is needed to full-scale machines, which are then most economically housed in a centralized, national center. The importance of the local availability of mid-range machines for researchers in software for parallel computers was noted in the Branscomb report (NSF, 1993).

• Provide resources to help complete the development and distribution of compilers, programming tools, and related infrastructure broadly usable by the software research community. Such infrastructure—which may be developed by individual research groups or by centers (such as the NSF science and technology centers)—has been crucial to rapid progress. For example, tools for the design of very large scale integrated (VLSI) circuits allowed many researchers to undertake VLSI designs. The committee notes that funding agencies should avoid turning related infrastructure development efforts into product development efforts.

• Seek improved integration of parallel computing hardware and software with communication networks, both in software and hardware research.

• Emphasize design and analysis of new algorithms for parallel computing, as well as implementation and evaluation of these algorithms on real parallel machines. Opportunities for development of new parallel algorithms exist in both scientific and information infrastructure-related applications. The theoretical performance and scaling efficiency of new algorithms need to be demonstrated by actual implementation and evaluation on parallel machines, first by computer scientists and then embedded in real end-user applications.

• Ensure that effective new algorithms for parallel computing are made widely available to end-user communities to assist in building applications.

Recommendation 3.1. Avoid funding the transfer ("porting") of existing commercial applications to new parallel computing machines unless there is a specific research need. Several existing applications enjoy widespread commercial use on large uniprocessor and vector machines; examples include third-party codes in chemistry, biomolecules, engineering fluid dynamics, deformable structures, and database access. It has been proposed by some that the HPCCI should fund transferring, or "porting," such applications to new types of parallel computers as a way to enhance the attractiveness of new parallel machines. The committee finds inappropriate the use of federal HPCCI funding for such porting of applications for several reasons. First, the algorithms used in these applications were designed for sequential or vector computing, and thus little new knowledge will be gained from merely porting existing applications to a parallel machine without redesigning the algorithms. Second, the open market will fund such transfers if a sufficient user base exists. Third, choosing whose application to transfer and to which machines will involve the HPCCI in picking winners from among many commercial vendors.

Although it recognizes that a federal agency might decide that one of its missions would best be served by porting an existing application to a parallel computer, the committee recommends that funding of such ports be justified on the basis of the agency mission and not as HPCCI research. The committee believes that it is legitimate for groups of agencies to work together to develop community codes for common applications needed by their several missions. Likewise, carrying out an HPCCI research program may require that applications be available on a particular parallel machine, in which case the transfer could be justified by the importance of the research it enabled. Finally, the committee also sees a legitimate reason to port existing applications for the purpose of evaluating machines within a research laboratory or university.

Recommendation 4. Stop direct HPCCI funding for development of commercial hardware by computer vendors and for "industrial stimulus" purchases of hardware. Maintain HPCCI support for precompetitive research in computer architecture; this work should be done in universities or in university-industry collaborations and should be driven by the needs of system and application software. The development and placement of parallel hardware to date was necessary to establish parallel computing as a viable alternative to sequential and vector computing. (The establishment of this paradigm is discussed throughout Chapter 2 and in Appendixes A and E.) Industry is now willing and able to improve on the base of ideas established by the HPCCI, at least for mainstream parallel machines (special government requirements are discussed below). Government development funds should no longer be spent in industry either to further refine parallel machines or to purchase machines as a stimulus for vendors.

The committee notes that use of HPCCI funds for these purposes has already decreased significantly, a trend that the committee supports.[2] Federal funding of hardware developments within companies should continue to decline, unless some special agency need demands the development of nonstandard hardware (e.g., a high-performance system for use on a ship or in an airplane, such as Intel Corporation's parallel Paragon computer made more rugged for military use, or for a highly specialized application). In such cases, agency mission funds, and not HPCCI funds, should be used.

Important precompetitive hardware research problems merit continued federal funding because the development of parallel computing architecture and gigabit networks will not be the final chapter in the continuing development of ever more powerful systems. The committee recommends that ongoing research efforts in hardware and architecture be based in academic and research institutions, possibly in collaboration with industry. Potential problems can be minimized if the research institution serves as the project lead, and if the research challenges rather than commercial development are the focus (Cohen and Noll, 1994). Not only do academic institutions have more freedom to think about longer-term issues, but they also stimulate technology transfer through publication and placement of graduates. The national experience supports a basic tenet of Vannevar Bush: publicly funded research carried out in universities produces excellence, diversity, fresh ideas, trained people, and technology transfer (OSRD and Bush, 1945). Commercial organizations, on the other hand, have powerful incentives to avoid distributing new ideas widely and may even impede the introduction of new technology when it competes with existing products.

To narrow the gap between parallel computing hardware capabilities and the software needed to use them, research on architecture should be driven by software and applications needs. Thus, further integration of application and system software needs into architecture research should be encouraged in any funding of architecture research.

Recommendation 5. Treat development of a teraflop computer as a research direction rather than a destination. The committee believes that federal investment in developing or purchasing machines to demonstrate raw scalability for its own sake is inappropriate, except as a focus for precompetitive, academic research. Instead, the focus should be on matching agencies' mission requirements to the emerging sustainable scalable architectures. Such architectures will very likely reach 1-teraflop capability before the end of this decade using 1,000 or so high-performance commercial microprocessors.

The goals of scalability over many sizes of machine and of demonstrating teraflop performance have been useful in pointing toward the use of mass-produced devices in large collections to solve complex computing tasks, but implementation of a machine of any specific size can be premature. Moreover, seeking a common design over a large size range is wasteful because the expensive communication paths required to harness large numbers of inexpensive processors together are inappropriate when scaled down to smaller machines with only a few processors. The pursuit of wide scalability may have deferred early consideration of shared-memory parallel computers, the type that today appears promising. In fact, the focus on teraflop capability detracts from other important aspects of high performance, such as memory and input/output systems, which are critical components of any high-performance system.

Advances in parallel architectures together with progress in the underlying integrated circuit technology will continue to provide improvements in performance/cost ratios that will naturally bring computing power to the teraflop level. Most industry analysts see the potential for single microprocessors with 1- to 2-gigaflop peak performance by the end of the decade. Combining 512 to 1024 such future microprocessors in a scalable system would create a teraflop capacity at roughly the price of today's supercomputers, with capabilities of tens of gigaflops possible. Supporting research into the key technologies needed to achieve and use scalable computing, combined with patience to see how the relative economics of computing power and communications interact, seems to this committee to be the most efficient approach to increasing performance.

The committee thus emphasizes that the HPCCI should treat the goal of teraflop performance as a milestone to be reached naturally by computer vendors in due course, not on a forced time scale. The HPCCI should continue to fund research on technologies that will contribute to reaching the goal. At some point in the near future a teraflop parallel machine will be built when some agencies' mission requirements correspond to a sufficiently economical commercial offering. Continued progress will naturally lead to machines much larger than a teraflop.

RECOMMENDATIONS ON NETWORKING AND INFORMATION INFRASTRUCTURE

The committee believes that the successes of the HPCCI in establishing scalable compute servers, investigating high-performance networks, and forming interdisciplinary teams of computer and application scientists are setting the stage for important new research to support enhancement of the nation's information infrastructure. An increased emphasis on the research needed to achieve such an infrastructure is desirable (CSTB, 1994d).

In fact, this shift has already begun; spending on networking and IITA activities accounted for nearly 50 percent of the HPCCI budget requested in FY 1995:[3] $177 million for the NREN and $282 million for IITA. This is a significant increase over the $114 million that was spent for NREN in FY 1993, the year prior to the addition of IITA. The committee believes that such a shift is appropriate.

Recommendation 6. Increase the HPCCI focus on communications and networking research, especially on the challenges inherent in scale and physical distribution. Advancing the nation's information infrastructure will put great demands on digital communications technology for providing broad access to services. Ensuring broad access poses a host of technical and economic questions for which existing solutions are inadequate. The committee recommends increased support for learning how to attach millions of users to a digital communications structure that provides a wide array of services and greater integration of services, and how to accommodate the demands that these users will generate using the novel applications enabled by such an information infrastructure.

Recommendation 7. Develop a research program to address the research challenges underlying our ability to build very large, reliable, high-performance, distributed information systems based on the existing HPCCI foundation. An improved infrastructure will need to offer capability to all facets of our economy on a scale not yet imagined, and no one yet anticipates all of the ways that users will use such an information infrastructure.

Improvements to the nation's information infrastructure and activities related to it have generated a level of public interest matched by only a few technology-based objectives. The committee is concerned that unrealistic expectations for availability and for the quality and range of services could encourage a short-term, product-oriented focus in funding research activities[4] that would not be in our country's best interest. Care should be taken to apprise policymakers and the public of the long time needed for development and wide-scale deployment of the services expected to be available through the information infrastructure.

The committee strongly recommends that the HPCCI remain focused on the basic research issues arising from desired improvements to the information infrastructure, evolving from its early emphasis on parallel, high-performance computing, high-performance networking, and scientific applications to the broader issues of connection, scale, distributed systems, and applications. The addition of the IITA area to the HPCCI was a key step in accelerating a shift in focus of the research community to the challenges of improving the nation's information infrastructure. The committee has identified three key areas where new emphasis is critical to supporting the research needs associated with the information infrastructure:

1. *Scalability.* While the HPCCI has emphasized large computing systems on the order of thousands of interacting computers, an enhanced, nationwide information infrastructure will require scaling to millions of users. In addition, the HPCCI has emphasized bringing the highest performance to bear on individual scientific applications, whereas improving the information infrastructure for the nation requires using the highest performance to meet the practical needs of millions of simultaneous users.

2. *Physical distribution and the problems it raises.* A better information infrastructure will emphasize geographical distribution with its limitations on bandwidth, increase in latency of communication, and additional challenges in secure and reliable communication. These challenges have been much less severe in localized high-performance parallel systems. Research on both distributed and parallel systems technology will be important in supporting this aspect of a national-scale information infrastructure.

3. *Innovative applications.* A shift should occur from a focus on specific Grand Challenge problems in science to well-formulated National Challenges that affect a wider segment of society. The committee sees an important role for development and demonstration of easily appreciated applications that will drive the technology of the information infrastructure.

Improving scalability and physical distribution requires investment in both:

• *Hardware and architecture,* including systems that efficiently handle a rich mix of text, images, and audio and video data; systems that provide cost-effective, high-bandwidth, end-to-end communications; and systems that provide information access to large numbers of users; and

• *Software,* including basic networking software for encryption, routing, flow control, and so on; tools for providing and building such capabilities as scheduling, bandwidth optimization, video handling, and service adaptation; and many others. This is the so-called "middleware."

The committee believes that building on the current HPCCI model of a coordinated program, avoiding central control, seems even more crucial for the IITA portion of the research program, because the challenges posed by an information infrastructure are inherently less well defined than those addressed by other components of the initiative. The committee is encouraged by the early development of cooperative research programs in IITA areas, such as the digital libraries program, which includes NSF, ARPA, and the National Aeronautics and Space Administration (NASA), and by recent attempts to identify topics for research, such as discussions among several hundred researchers and others at a workshop in early 1994 (Vernon et al., 1994).

Recommendation 8. Ensure that research programs focusing on the National Challenges contribute to the development of information infrastructure technologies as well as to the development of new applications and paradigms. The National Challenges incorporate socially significant problems of national importance that can also drive the development of information infrastructure. Hardware and software researchers should play a major role in these projects to facilitate progress and to improve the communication with researchers developing basic technologies for the information infrastructure. Awards to address the National Challenges should reflect the importance of the area as well as the research team's strength in both the applications and the underlying technologies. The dual emphasis recommended by the committee contrasts with the narrower focus on scientific results that has driven many of the Grand Challenge projects.

Because the National Challenges as currently defined are too broad and vague to offer specific targets for large-scale research, the notion of establishing testbeds for a complete national challenge is premature. Instead, research funding agencies should regard the National Challenges as general areas from which to select specific projects for limited-scale testbeds or focused software research projects. Particular areas in which a focused research target can be identified (e.g., the ARPA-NSF-NASA digital library testbeds) may be appropriate for slightly higher funding, but the committee believes that very large scale applications development is premature. At this early stage, letting "a thousand flowers bloom" will provide a better pay-back than funding a few large or full-scale deployments. (Box A.3 and related text in Appendix A give more information on the National Challenges.)

RECOMMENDATIONS ON THE SUPERCOMPUTER CENTERS AND GRAND CHALLENGE PROGRAM

The four NSF supercomputer centers are the largest single element of the FY 1995 HPCCI implementation plan in dollars ($76 million, or 6.6 percent of the requested FY 1995 HPCCI budget) and the largest infrastructure project in the initiative. The centers—which give users access to a broad array of powerful tools ranging from highly innovative to mature—are a significant national resource for gaining knowledge, experience, and capability. Thanks to their leadership, high-performance computing and communications are now widely accepted as an important tool in academia, industry, and commerce.

The centers have played a major role in establishing parallel computing as a full partner with the prior paradigms of scalar and vector computing. They have contributed by providing access to state-of-the-art computing facilities to a broad range of users. As new large-scale architectures appear, the centers stimulate their early use by providing access to these architectures and by educating and training users. (Appendix E details the accomplishments of the NSF centers and of their national user base.)

The committee recognizes that advanced computation is an important tool for scientists and engineers and that support for adequate computer access must be a part of the NSF research program in all disciplines. The committee also sees value in providing large-scale, centralized computing, storage, and visualization resources that can provide unique capabilities. How such resources should be funded and what the long-term role of the centers should be with respect to both new and maturing computing architectures are critical questions that NSF should reexamine in detail, perhaps via the newly announced Ad Hoc Task Force on the Future of the NSF Supercomputer Centers Program. For example, much of the general access to computing resources at the centers is provided on maturing architectures. Neither the quality of the science performed by the users of such technology nor the appropriateness of NSF funding for such general access is in question. The committee did not consider the appropriate overall funding level for the centers. Nonetheless, the committee does question the exclusive use by the NSF of HPCCI-specific funds for support of general computing access, which in itself does not simultaneously help drive the development of high-performance computing and communications technology.

In this regard, NSF follows a different approach to funding its supercomputer centers than do NASA and the Department of Energy (DOE), where HPCCI funds are used only to support the exploration and use of new computing architectures, while non-HPCCI funds are used to support general access. The committee believes that DOE's and NASA's approach to funding general access should be followed across the agencies. Also, as the committee points out in Recommendation 12, including all of the NSF supercomputer centers' funding under HPCCI could cause major disruption to the centers' national mission should the HPCCI be altered significantly.

Recommendation 9. The mission of the National Science Foundation supercomputer centers remains important, but the NSF should continue to evaluate new directions, alternative funding mechanisms, new administrative structures, and the overall program level of the centers. NSF could continue funding of the centers at the current level or alter that level, but it should continue using HPCCI funds to support applications that contribute to the evolution of the underlying computing and communications technologies, while support for general access by application scientists to maturing architectures should come increasingly from non-HPCCI funds.

Examination of the supercomputer centers program should include identification of:

- Emerging new roles for the centers in supporting changing national needs; and
- Future funding mechanisms, including charging mechanisms and funding coupled to disciplinary directorates.

In addition to enabling high-performance scientific computing, several of the NSF centers have developed new software technologies that have significantly affected other parts of the HPCCI. The most obvious of these is the recently developed Mosaic World Wide Web browser. The committee recommends that NSF continue to take a broad view of the centers' mission of providing access to HPCCI resources, including, but clearly not limited to, participating in research needed for improved software for parallel machines and for enhancement of the nation's information infrastructure. The centers, and the researchers who use their facilities, should compete for research funds by the normal means established by the funding agencies.

Recommendation 10. The Grand Challenge program is an innovative approach to creating interdisciplinary and multi-institutional scientific research teams; however, continued use of HPCCI funds is appropriate only when the research contributes significantly to the development of new high-performance computing and communications hardware or software. Grand Challenge projects funded under the HPCCI should be evaluated on the basis of their contributions both to high-performance computing and communications and to the application area. The Grand Challenge problems are sufficiently large and complex and the research teams addressing them are capable enough to exercise the parallel computing technology thoroughly and to test its capability. These efforts have been supported under the HPCCI as a valid way to involve real users in parallel computing, but as parallel computing becomes an established tool, the need to use the HPCCI to stimulate the user community will decrease. Furthermore, the use of high-performance computing will become more pervasive, making it unreasonable to include all such programs with the HPCCI.

The committee recommends completion of the initial Grand Challenges as planned over the next few years. Currently, although the scientific disciplines are providing major funding for Grand Challenge projects (e.g., more than 50 percent of requested FY 1995 funds for NSF Grand Challenges come from the scientific and engineering research directorates), virtually all of the Grand Challenge funding is labeled HPCCI. The committee urges that any follow-on funding of Grand Challenges include a significant and growing fraction of non-HPCCI scientific disciplinary funds. This will limit the selection to tasks whose scientific interest justifies their cost, in competition with other research in their respective disciplines.

The committee sees an ongoing value from the strong interaction between challenging applications and new architectures and software systems and from cooperation between computer and computational scientists—a number of the Grand Challenge teams have demonstrated that collaboration can lead to advances in both computing and the particular scientific discipline involved. Partial funding of applications research that contributes to the development of new hardware and software systems is a legitimate use of HPCCI funds. Such activities must be evaluated on the basis of their contributions both to high-performance computing and communications technologies and to the application area.

RECOMMENDATIONS ON COORDINATION AND PROGRAM MANAGEMENT IN THE HPCCI

Recommendation 11. Strengthen the HPCCI National Coordination Office (NCO) while retaining the cooperative structure of the HPCCI and increasing the opportunity for external input. As the committee pointed out in its interim report (CSTB, 1994c, p. 9), the dimensions of the need for clear communication about the HPCCI have recently become apparent: congressional oversight activities and other indicators suggest that the HPCCI is of concern to a growing constituency and that often a variety of audiences need detailed explanations of it. Such an effort will add substantially to the work of the NCO, which has been headed by a half-time, permanent-position director who holds a concurrent, half-time appointment as director of the National Library of Medicine (NLM).[5] The other NCO staff positions are a mix of permanent positions, contract positions, and temporary positions filled by individuals on loan from other federal agencies for limited periods of time, often no more than 1 year.[6]

Although the NCO reports to the Office of Science and Technology Policy (OSTP) on programmatic matters, administrative functions such as office space, salaries, and benefits have been handled through the National Institutes of Health. The temporary nature of some of the NCO positions jeopardizes continuity and cumulative insight. Further, limited staff resources raise questions about the NCO's capacity to meet the challenge of the growing volume, complexity, and urgency of the outreach efforts needed for the initiative (CSTB, 1994c, p. 9).

The NCO serves an important coordination and communication function both among agencies of the government and between the agencies, Congress, industry, and the public. It is to the credit of the NCO staff that the HPCCI has been an effective model of interagency collaboration. In recommending a strengthening of the NCO, the committee strongly endorses the current NCO's role of supporting the mission agencies rather than directing them. The committee believes that it is vital that direction of the HPCCI remain in the agencies.

By avoiding actual direction the NCO leaves mission judgments in the hands of responsible agency officials who are accountable for the allocation of their resources. By avoiding the appearance of direction the NCO encourages an appropriate diversity of research projects as each agency capitalizes on its best ideas. Mission agencies cooperate effectively with each other and with the NCO precisely because it does not threaten their autonomy. This cooperation could easily vanish were the NCO seen as functioning with too heavy a hand. The committee believes that the value of interagency cooperation outweighs the potential benefits that might be gained through more centralized management of the HPCCI (CSTB, 1994c, p. 8).

The committee strongly recommends retaining the model of a cooperative and coordinated interagency program. Some individuals and organizations have expressed concern about the lack of centralized management of the HPCCI. However, the committee believes that the current cooperative structure is one of the initiative's strengths, providing room for diversity of thought and action. Such diversity is essential to progress, because no one manager or agency has a monopoly on the right ideas for the future of computing and communications. Central management of the HPCCI could focus its activities too narrowly, as well as lead to reduced interest in the program by agencies that found that the centralized agenda no longer matched their interests.[7]

The committee believes that government investment in information technology research has often enjoyed first-class leadership. Program officers with vision have supported innovative ideas, leading to later successes. The committee emphasizes that the best method for making continued research investment is to continue to attract highly competent program officers and to give them the flexibility to develop effective programs. In the past, this approach has yielded solid returns on the research investment. Furthermore, it has encouraged necessary diversity in the research program, thus increasing opportunities for unexpected discoveries and ensuring a broad perspective in addressing problems.

Recommendation 11.1. Immediately appoint the congressionally mandated advisory committee intended to provide broad-based, active input to the HPCCI, or provide an effective alternative. The HPCCI could be improved by input from and review by an advisory committee with balanced representation from industry and academia, including current and potential users and developers of high-performance computing and communications. If appointment of such a committee is not feasible, some alternate mechanism should soon be developed to provide similar input. The committee is aware of the recent increases in the number of advisory committees, as well as the danger of having too many committees. Thus, the committee recommends that the HPCCI advisory committee have a well-defined role focusing primarily on providing external input into the coordination and planning for the HPCCI.

Recommendation 11.2. Appoint an individual to be a full-time coordinator, program spokesperson, and advocate for the HPCCI. Having a part-time NCO director has served well to this point, but the broadening of the HPCCI demands leadership unencumbered by other major responsibilities. A full-time person could either direct the NCO or could report to the director and would work to strengthen the ties between the HPCCI, industry, the Congress, and the public. The committee uses the word "coordinator" rather than "manager" to emphasize the need for coordination and communication that avoid usurping the authority of the mission agencies. The NCO should remain within the OSTP structure.

Recommendation 12. Place projects in the HPCCI only if they match well to its objectives. A number of preexisting agency programs have entered the HPCCI. Such administrative changes make the HPCCI budget appear to grow faster than the real growth of investment in high-performance computing and communications. Some of these programs exactly match the goals of the HPCCI and are properly included. Others are only marginally relevant and might better be placed elsewhere in agency budgets. The committee sees the possibility of a long-term danger to important programs, such as basic research in computing within NSF and ARPA, should the HPCCI end.

Recommendation 12.1. Federal research funding agencies should promptly document the extent to which HPCCI funding is supporting important long-term research areas whose future funding should be independent of the future of the HPCCI. The committee found that many research areas predating the HPCCI and related only partly to its goals are now under the

HPCCI umbrella. Although encouraging important research areas to include and even focus on HPCCI-related components, the process of coding all funding in a research area as high-performance computing and communications can be dangerous. In many cases, areas were recoded as high-performance computing and communications without receiving an increase in funds. The danger in this process is that changes in the direction or level of funding for the HPCCI could lead to unintentional changes in the funding levels of important research areas, even if they are largely unrelated to the HPCCI and even if they have received none of the HPCCI incremental funding!

This problem is particularly acute at NSF, where nearly all of the funding in the Computer and Information Science and Engineering directorate is coded as HPCCI funding. Given that NSF is not a mission agency and is investigator-driven, this approach seems shortsighted. NSF would have to retain funding for computer science research even in the absence of the HPCCI. Ongoing funding of important research areas in computer science will be critical to the nation's future, independent of the future of the HPCCI.

Recommendation 13. Base mission agency computer procurements on mission needs only, and encourage making equipment procurement decisions at the lowest practical management level. To stimulate the use of parallel computing early in the HPCCI's 5-year time frame, it has been appropriate and necessary to place into service a reasonable number of highly parallel machines for serious algorithm and software development. Early development of an adequate base of parallel computers was essential to shifting the attention of industry and research organizations toward parallel computing. Now, however, it is more appropriate to base procurement of computer hardware on mission needs only. One program that claims to have done so already is the Defense High Performance Computing Modernization Program. The committee applauds modernization of the computing facilities available to Department of Defense organizations and the mission-driven nature of the procurement process, which should be established in all agencies.

Each agency has responsibility for its own budget and its own requirements. The committee believes that agencies should base procurements of computing equipment on their needs and budget constraints. Agencies should be free to purchase parallel computers when they suit agency needs. Individual agencies can balance the cost of obtaining applications against the cost of computing equipment so as to best match procurements to their requirements. Parallel computing is now mature enough to be considered a viable alternative to other forms of computing and may deliver suitable computing power at less cost than other architectures.

Although the committee firmly recommends that computer purchases be guided by mission needs, it also sees a role for collaboration between mission agencies and industrial or university parallel computing consortia. Direct agency responsibility for missions, budgets, and equipment purchases can be reconciled with the advantages of group action through participation in appropriate consortia. For example, the NSF centers have proven valuable for offering exploratory experience with high-performance computing, and it is encouraging to see industrial-academic consortia forming to explore parallel computing. The committee encourages mission agencies to participate with the NSF centers and other parallel computing consortia. Such participation offers knowledge at low cost and leads ultimately to more cost-effective procurements.

The committee's recommendation that equipment be selected at the lowest practical management level applies equally to government agencies and to government contractors. The direct manager of a computing facility is charged with making it work and will do that task best if allowed to select equipment that matches the facility's needs. The committee believes that agency-wide procurement of standard brands, while promoting collaboration, can weaken the responsibility of the user organizations. Likewise, it has generally been best for an agency to specify the results it wants and to leave the choice of specific equipment to the contractor.[8] Delegating equipment selection not only saves top-level agency decision-making resources but also places responsibility for purchase decisions firmly in the hands of the managers who must deliver results.

COMMENTS RELATING THIS REPORT'S RECOMMENDATIONS FOR HIGH-PERFORMANCE COMPUTING AND COMMUNICATIONS RESEARCH TO ADMINISTRATION PRIORITIES

This report's recommendations broadly address much of the computer science and engineering research being conducted today, as well as the HPCCI specifically. In a May 1994 memorandum from the director of the Office of Management and Budget to all agency heads, the administration outlined its priorities for U.S. research and development in general. Box 3.1 briefly compares applicable parts of that memorandum to the positions taken and actions recommended in this report of the Committee to Study High Performance Computing and Communications.

BOX 3.1 Comparison of Administration Priorities for Harnessing Information Technology to Committee Recommendations in This Report

Computing Systems

"The development of scalable systems with the input/output capabilities, mass storage systems, real-time services, and information security features needed to build and fully utilize the National Information Infrastructure (NII) should be emphasized. High performance computing systems capable of 10^{12} operations per second (a teraflop) on technical problems will be achieved by FY 1997. Emphasis should be placed on advances in information storage media for both high and low end applications; systems integration of clustered workstations and large parallel systems; development of advanced tools and processes for the design and prototyping of faster semiconductor devices; and research on nanotechnology, photonics, flat panel displays, and integrated micro-electrical-mechanical devices."

The Committee on High Performance Computing and Communications recommends continuing the focus on high-performance parallel computing, but decreasing the emphasis on achieving a teraflop computing system on a specific time scale. The committee agrees that scalable high-performance computing and communications technology that supports the nation's emerging information infrastructure is important. The committee also recommends increased emphasis on the support of communications within new computer systems.

Networking and Communications

"It will be necessary to support the development of the networking technology required for the deployment of national gigabit speed networks incorporating heterogeneous carriers including satellite and wireless capability. This means serving hundreds of millions of users and demonstrating mobile and wireless capability. It includes the development of interoperability concepts and technologies and the integration of computers, televisions, telephones, wireless telecommunications and satellites."

The committee thoroughly agrees.

continues

BOX 3.1—*continued*

Software, Algorithms, and Basic Research

> "The United States should conduct basic research to support the computational requirements of new computing paradigms. There is a need for new methods for data authentication and software verification and validation. The development of tools and techniques to enable assembly of systems from inexpensive, versatile, reusable software components is required."

The committee's recommendations emphasize the importance of a complete program of basic research in computer science and underscore the importance of research on software and algorithms to make the best use of new computing paradigms.

Information Infrastructure Services

> "Access to and utilization of the NII will require services, tools, and interfaces that facilitate a wide range of applications. These include registries, directories, navigation and resource discovery tools, data interchange formats, and other information services that help users find and query services and components in distributed repositories. There will have to be new types of human-computer access and the development of improved collaborative software, groupware, and authoring tools for multimedia will be important. Equally important are the development of privacy and security technologies and integrated information and monitoring systems."

The committee enthusiastically agrees.

Human-Computer Interaction

> "New products and applications are enabled by those hardware and software technologies that will allow every American to use easily the NII. Development and use of the following should be advanced: virtual reality; simulation; flat-panel displays; video and high definition systems; three-dimensional sound, speech interfaces, and vision."

The committee did not study human-computer interaction and specific related areas for research, although these are certainly a key part of a broad research program on information infrastructure.

Computing and Communications Applications

> "The FY 1996 R&D budget should advance applications of high-performance computing and the NII. The Federal High-performance Computing and Communications Program is helping to develop the technologies and techniques needed to solve critical research problems that require more advanced computers, storage devices, algorithms, and software tools. Additional effort is needed to accelerate the transfer of these technologies from the laboratory to the marketplace."

The committee recommends that applications be funded increasingly from outside the HPCCI, especially as the technology underlying the application becomes mature. HPCCI funds should focus research support on applications that affect the base computing and communication technologies, as well as solve new applications problems. The committee recommends that such a policy be followed in funding work on the Grand Challenges and the emerging National Challenges.

SOURCE: Panetta (1994), pp. 10-11.

NOTES

1. See the subsections "Programming" and "Algorithms" in Appendix A for a discussion of development and achievements to date.

2. Based on briefings to the committee by Anita Jones (Department of Defense); Duane Adams, Howard Frank, and John Toole (Advanced Research Projects Agency); and Victor Reis (Department of Energy).

3. See NCO (1994), p. 15. Note that figures represent the President's requested budget authority for FY 1995. Actual appropriated levels were not available at press time. Because the HPCCI is synthesized as a cross-cutting multiagency initiative, there is no direct "HPCCI appropriation."

4. This risk is illustrated in the GAO examples of standards setting and other nonresearch activities under the HPCCI umbrella.

5. A January 6, 1995, press release from the Office of Science and Technology Policy announced the resignation of the NCO's director, Donald A.B. Lindberg. Lindberg, requesting that a successor be named when his current 2-year term ends, recommended that a full-time director be appointed at this point in the evolution of the HPCCI.

6. Letter dated August 8, 1994, to Marjory Blumenthal (CSTB) from Donald A.B. Lindberg (NCO/NLM) in response to the committee's interim report (CSTB, 1994c).

7. The committee shares OSTP Director John Gibbons' concerns about the centralized management advocated by GAO (1994, p. 34).

8. The committee notes the extreme fruitfulness of this model in the hands of the late Sidney Fernbach of DOE's Lawrence Livermore National Laboratory, who for a generation kept his laboratory at the forefront of computing and at the same time helped to stimulate the development of generations of supercomputers.

Bibliography

Anthes, Gary H. 1994. "Cray Envisions New Frontier," *Computerworld,* July 18, p. 121.

Anthes, Gary H., and Mitch Betts. 1994. "R&D: Measure of Success," *Computerworld,* November 14, p. 32.

Browder, Felix E. 1992. "Of Time, Intelligence, and Institutions," *Dædalus* 121(1 Winter):105-110.

Carlton, Jim. 1994. "Makers of PCs Had Very, Very Happy Holiday," *Wall Street Journal,* December 27, pp. B1 and B4.

Carnevale, Mary Lu. 1994. "U.S. Awards Grants to Spur Data Network," *Wall Street Journal,* October 13, p. B6.

Cohen, Linda R., and Roger G. Noll. 1994. "Privatizing Public Research," *Scientific American* 271(3):72-77.

Commission on Physical Sciences, Mathematics, and Applications (CPSMA); National Research Council. 1994. *Quantitative Assessments of the Physical and Mathematical Sciences: A Summary of Lessons Learned.* National Academy Press, Washington, D.C.

Committee on Information and Communication (CIC). 1994. *High Performance Computing and Communications: Technology for the National Information Infrastructure, Supplement to the President's Fiscal Year 1995 Budget.* National Science and Technology Council, Washington, D.C.

Computer and Business Equipment Manufacturers Association (CBEMA). 1994. *Information Technology Industry Data Book 1960-2004.* Computer and Business Equipment Manufacturers Association, Washington, D.C.

Computer Science and Technology Board (CSTB), National Research Council. 1988. *The National Challenge in Computer Science and Technology.* National Academy Press, Washington, D.C.

Computer Science and Telecommunications Board (CSTB), National Research Council. 1992. *Computing the Future: A Broader Agenda for Computer Science and Engineering.* National Academy Press, Washington, D.C.

Computer Science and Telecommunications Board (CSTB), National Research Council. 1993. *National Collaboratories: Applying Information Technology for Scientific Research.* National Academy Press, Washington, D.C.

Computer Science and Telecommunications Board (CSTB), National Research Council. 1994a. *Academic Careers for Experimental Computer Scientists and Engineers.* National Academy Press, Washington, D.C.

Computer Science and Telecommunications Board (CSTB), National Research Council. 1994b. *Information Technology in the Service Society: A Twenty-first Century Lever.* National Academy Press, Washington, D.C.

Computer Science and Telecommunications Board (CSTB), National Research Council. 1994c. *Interim Report on the Status of the High Performance Computing and Communications Initiative.* Computer Science and Telecommunications Board, Washington, D.C.

Computer Science and Telecommunications Board (CSTB), National Research Council. 1994d. *Realizing the Information Future: The Internet and Beyond.* National Academy Press, Washington, D.C.

Computer Science and Telecommunications Board (CSTB), National Research Council. 1994e. *Research Recommendations to Facilitate Distributed Work.* National Academy Press, Washington, D.C.

Computer Science and Telecommunications Board (CSTB), National Research Council. 1995. *Information Technology for Manufacturing: A Research Agenda.* National Academy Press, Washington, D.C., in press.

Computer Select. 1994. *Data Sources Report.* Ziff Communications Company, New York, December.

Computer Systems Policy Project (CSPP). 1991. *Expanding the Vision of High Performance Computing and Communications: Linking America for the Future.* Computer Systems Policy Project, Washington, D.C., December 3.

Computer Systems Policy Project (CSPP). 1993. *Perspectives on the National Information Infrastructure: CSPP's Vision and Recommendations for Action.* Computer Systems Policy Project, Washington, D.C.

Computer Systems Policy Project (CSPP). 1994. *Perspectives on the National Information Infrastructure: Accelerating the Development and Deployment of NII Technologies.* Computer Systems Policy Project, Washington, D.C.

Congressional Budget Office (CBO). 1993. *Promoting High-Performance Computing and Communications.* U.S. Government Printing Office, Washington, D.C., June.

Corcoran, Elizabeth. 1994. "The Changing Role of U.S. Corporate Research Labs," *Research-Technology Management* 37(4):14-20.

Council on Competitiveness. 1991. *Gaining New Ground: Technology Priorities for America's Future.* Council on Competitiveness, Washington, D.C.

Coy, Peter. 1993. "R&D Scoreboard: In the Labs, the Fight to Spend Less, Get More," *Business Week*, June 28, pp. 102-124.

Deng, Yuefan, James Glimm, and David H. Sharp. 1992. "Perspectives on Parallel Computing," *Dœdalus* 121(1 Winter):31-52.

Economides, Nicholas, and C. Himmelberg. 1994. "Critical Mass and Network Size," presented at the Telecommunications Policy Research Conference, Solomons Island, Md., October 1-3.

Faltermayer, Edmund. 1993. "Invest or Die," *Fortune* 127(4):42-52.

Federal Coordinating Council for Science, Engineering, and Technology (FCCSET), Office of Science and Technology Policy. 1991. *Grand Challenges: High Performance Computing and Communications, The FY 1992 U.S. Research and Development Program.* Committee on Physical, Mathematical, and Engineering Sciences, Office of Science and Technology Policy, Washington, D.C., February 5.

Federal Coordinating Council for Science, Engineering, and Technology (FCCSET), Office of Science and Technology Policy. 1992. *Grand Challenges 1993: High Performance Computing and Communications, The FY 1993 U.S. Research and Development Program.* Committee on Physical, Mathematical, and Engineering Sciences, Office of Science and Technology Policy, Washington, D.C.

Federal Coordinating Council for Science, Engineering, and Technology (FCCSET), Office of Science and Technology Policy. 1993. *FCCSET Initiatives in the FY 1994 Budget.* Office of Science and Technology Policy, Washington, D.C., April 8.

Federal Coordinating Council for Science, Engineering, and Technology (FCCSET), Office of Science and Technology Policy. 1994. *High Performance Computing and Communications: Toward a National Information Infrastructure.* Committee on Physical, Mathematical, and Engineering Sciences, Office of Science and Technology Policy, Washington, D.C.

Feldman, Jerome A., and William R. Sutherland. 1979. "Rejuvenating Experimental Computer Science," *Communications of the ACM*, September, pp. 497-502.

Flamm, Kenneth. 1987. *Targeting the Computer: Government Support and International Competition.* Brookings Institution, Washington, D.C.

Flamm, Kenneth. 1988. *Creating the Computer: Government, Industry, and High Technology.* Brookings Institution, Washington, D.C.

Forrester Research Inc. 1994. "Home PCs: The Golden Age," *The Forrester Report,* October.

Furht, Borko. 1994. "Parallel Computing: Glory and Collapse," *Computer* 27(11):74-75.

Geppert, Linda. 1994. "Industrial R&D: The New Priorities," *IEEE Spectrum* 31(9):30-41.

Goldfarb, Debra. 1994. *Workstations and High-Performance Systems: Primary Applications for High-Performance Computers.* International Data Corporation, Framingham, Mass.

Gore, Jr., Albert. 1993. *From Red Tape to Results, Creating a Government That Works Better & Costs Less: Reengineering Through Information Technology, Accompanying Report of the National Performance Review.* U.S. Government Printing Office, Washington, D.C., September.

Hamilton, Alexander. 1791. "Report [to the Congress] on Manufactures," in M.J. Frisch (ed.), *Selected Writings and Speeches of Alexander Hamilton*, pp. 277-318. American Enterprise Institute for Public Policy Research, Washington, D.C., and London.

Hillis, W. Daniel. 1992. "What Is Massively Parallel Computing, and Why Is It Important?" *Dædalus* 121(1 Winter):1-15.

Holcomb, Lee B. 1994. Statement before the House Committee on Science, Space, and Technology: Subcommittee on Science, May 10.

Information Infrastructure Task Force. 1993. *The National Information Infrastructure: Agenda for Action.* Information Infrastructure Task Force, Washington, D.C., September 15.

International Business Machines Corporation. 1954. *Preliminary Report: Specifications for the IBM Mathematical FORmula TRANslating System, FORTRAN.* Programming Research Group, Applied Science Division. International Business Machines, New York.

International Business Machines Corporation. 1956. *The FORTRAN Automatic Coding System for the IBM 704 EDPM (Programmer's Reference Manual).* International Business Machines, New York.

Kahaner, David K. 1994a. "Fujitsu Parallel Computing Workshop, 11/94, Kawasaki," November 28, distributed electronically.

Kahaner, David. 1994b. "Hitachi Parallel Computer Announcement," April 14, distributed electronically.

Kahaner, David K. 1994c. "Japanese Supercomputer Purchases," September 2, distributed electronically.

Kaufmann III, William J., and Larry L. Smarr. 1993. *Supercomputing and the Transformation of Science.* Scientific American Library, New York.

Lewis, Ted. 1994. "Supercomputers Ain't So Super," *Computer* 27(11):5-6.

Lindberg, Donald A.B. 1994. Statement before the House Committee on Science, Space, and Technology: Subcommittee on Science, May 10.

Markoff, John. 1995. "Digital Devices Draw Consumers," *New York Times,* January 7, pp. 39 and 50.

National Coordination Office (NCO) for High Performance Computing and Communications. 1993. *Technology Transfer Activities Within the Federal High Performance Computing and Communications Program.* NCO HPCC 93-01. National Coordination Office for High Performance Computing and Communications, Bethesda, Md., April.

National Coordination Office (NCO) for High Performance Computing and Communications, Office of Science and Technology Policy. 1994. *FY 1995 Implementation Plan.* National Coordination Office for High Performance Computing and Communications, Bethesda, Md.

National Science and Technology Council (NSTC). 1994a. "Program Description." Electronics Subcommittee, Civilian Industrial Technology Committee, National Science and Technology Council, Washington, D.C.

National Science and Technology Council (NSTC). 1994b. *Science in the National Interest.* National Science and Technology Council, Washington, D.C., August.

National Science Foundation (NSF). 1993. *Research on Digital Libraries: Announcement.* NSF 93-141. National Science Foundation, Washington, D.C.

National Science Foundation (NSF). 1994. *Research Priorities in Networking and Communications.* Report to the NSF Division of Networking and Communications Research and Infrastructure by Members of the Workshop held May 12-14, 1994, Airlie House, Va.

Nelson, David. 1994. Statement before the House Committee on Science, Space, and Technology: Subcommittee on Science, May 10.

New York Times. 1994. "Experimental Fusion Reactor at Princeton Sets a Record," November 9, p. A22.

NSF Blue Ribbon Panel on High Performance Computing. 1993. *From Desktop to Teraflop: Exploiting the U.S. Lead in High Performance Computing.* National Science Foundation, Arlington, Va., August.

Office of Science and Technology Policy. 1989. *The Federal High Peformance Computing Program.* Executive Office of the President, September 8.

Office of Scientific Research and Development (OSRD) and Vannevar Bush. 1945. *Science: The Endless Frontier.* U.S. Government Printing Office, Washington, D.C.

Panetta, Leon E. 1994. "Memorandum for the Heads of Departments and Agencies: FY 1996 Research and Development (R&D) Priorities." Office of Management and Budget, Washington, D.C., May 12.

Parker-Smith, Norris (editor at large). 1994a. "Hi-demand, Lo-price Dilemma for Scalable Vendors," *HPCwire* 3(45):Article 1518 (distributed electronically).

Parker-Smith, Norris (editor at large). 1994b. "NEC Joins Parallel Parade with Wide Range of CMOS Systems," *HPCwire* 3(45, November 11):Article 1513, distributed electronically.

Patterson, David A., and John L. Hennessy. 1994. *Computer Organization and Design: The Hardware/Software Interface.* Morgan Kaufmann Publishers, San Mateo, Calif.

Rensberger, Boyce. 1994. "Scientific Ranks Outpace Funds: Imbalance May Put Nation's Technological Primacy at Risk." *Washington Post,* December 25, pp. A1 and A20.

Riggs, Brian. 1994. "IBM, Sun Vie for Thinking Machines' MPP Technology," *Computer* 27(12):9.

Roach, Stephen S. 1994. "Economics Inside the U.S. Economy," *U.S. Investment Research.* Morgan Stanley, New York, July 15.

Rowell, Jan. 1994. "ORNL's Ken Kliewer on How to Put the Sizzle Back in HPCC," *HPCwire* 3(47, December 2):Article 9023, distributed electronically.

Schatz, Bruce R., and Joseph B. Hardin. 1994. "NCSA Mosaic and the World Wide Web: Global Hypermedia Protocols for the Internet," *Science* 265(12 August):895-901.

Schwartz, Jacob T. 1992. "America's Economic-Technological Agenda for the 1990s," *Dœdalus* 121(1, Winter):139-165.

Sikorovsky, Elizabeth. 1994. "ARPA Issues $85M Networking Bonanza," *Federal Computer Week,* April 25, p. 3.

Snell, Monica. 1994. "Supercomputing: Same Name, Different Game," *Computer* 27(11):6-7.

Toole, John C. 1994. Statement before the House Committee on Science, Space, and Technology: Subcommittee on Science, May 10.

U.S. Department of Commerce (DOC), International Trade Administration. 1994. *U.S. Industrial Outlook, 1994.* U.S. Government Printing Office, Washington, D.C.

U.S. Department of Defense. 1960. *COBOL: Initial Specifications for a Common Business Oriented Language.* U.S. Government Printing Office, Washington, D.C.

U.S. Department of Defense. 1988. *Bolstering Defense Industrial Competitiveness: Report to the Secretary of Defense by the Undersecretary of Defense (Acquisition).* Department of Defense, Washington, D.C.

U.S. General Accounting Office (GAO). 1993. *High Performance Computing: Advanced Research Projects Agency Should Do More to Foster Program Goals.* U.S. General Accounting Office, Washington, D.C., May.

U.S. General Accounting Office (GAO). 1994. *High Performance Computing and Communications: New Program Direction Would Benefit from a More Focused Effort.* GAO/AIMD-95-6. U.S. General Accounting Office, Washington, D.C., November.

Vernon, Mary K., Edward D. Lazowska, and Stewart D. Personick (eds.). 1994. *R&D for the NII: Technical Challenges.* Report of a workshop held February 28 and March 1, 1994, in Gaithersburg, Md. EDUCOM, Washington, D.C.

Vishkin, Uzi (ed.). 1994. *Developing a Computer Science Agenda for High-Performance Computing.* ACM Press, New York.

Zatner, Aaron. 1994. "Sinking Machines," *Boston Globe,* September 6, pp. 21-25.

Appendixes

A
The High Performance Computing and Communications Initiative: Background

THE TECHNICAL-ECONOMIC IMPERATIVE FOR PARALLEL COMPUTING

The United States Needs More Powerful Computers and Communications

The High Performance Computing and Communications Initiative (HPCCI) addresses demanding applications in many diverse segments of the nation's economy and society. In information technology, government has often had to solve larger problems earlier than other sections of society. Government and the rest of society, however, have mostly the same applications, and all find their current applications growing in size, complexity, and mission centrality. All sectors are alike in their demands for continual improvement in computer speed, memory size, communications bandwidth, and large-scale switching. As more power becomes increasingly available and economical, new high-value applications become feasible. In recent decades, for example, inexpensive computer power has enabled magnetic resonance imaging, hurricane prediction, and sophisticated materials design. Box A.1 lists additional selected examples of recent and potential applications of high-performance computing and communications technologies. (See also Appendix D for a list of applications and activities associated with the "National Challenges" and Appendix E for an outline of supercomputing applications.)

BOX A.1 Examples of Important Applications of High-Performance Computing and Communications Technologies

- Continuous, on-line processing of millions of financial transactions
- Understanding of human joint mechanics
- Modeling of blood circulation in the human heart
- Prediction and modeling of severe storms
- Oil reservoir modeling
- Design of aerospace vehicles
- Linking of researchers and science classrooms
- Digital libraries
- Improved access to government information

Conventional Supercomputers Face Cost Barriers

For four decades and over six computer generations, there has been a countable demand, much of it arising from defense needs, for a few score to a few hundred supercomputers, machines built to be as fast as the state of the art would allow. These machines have cost from $5 million to $25 million each (in *current* dollars). The small market size has always meant that a large part of the per-machine cost has been development cost, tens to hundreds of millions of dollars. Such products are peculiarly susceptible to cost-rise, market-drop spirals.

As supercomputers have become faster, they have become ever more difficult and costly to design, build, and maintain. Conventional supercomputers use exotic electronic components, many of which have few other uses. Because of the limited supercomputer market, these components are manufactured in small quantities at correspondingly high cost. Increasingly, this cost is capital cost for the special manufacturing processes required, and development cost for pushing the state of the component and circuit art.

Moreover, supercomputers' large central memories require high bandwidth and fast circuits. The speed and complexity of the processors and memories demand special wiring. Supercomputers require expensive cooling systems and consume large amounts of electrical power. Thoughtful prediction shows that supercomputers face nonlinear cost increases for designing and developing entirely new circuits, chip processes, capital equipment, specialized software, and the machines themselves.

At the same time, the end of the Cold War has eliminated much of the historical market for speed at any cost. Many observers believe we are at, or within one machine generation of, the end of the specialized-technology supercomputer line.

Small Computers Are Becoming Faster, Cheaper, and More Widely Used

Meanwhile the opposite cost-volume spiral is occurring in microcomputers. Mass-production of integrated circuits yields single-chip microprocessors of surprising power, particularly in comparison to their cost. The economics of the industry mean that it is less expensive to build more transistors than to build faster transistors. The per-transistor price of each of the millions of transistors in mass-produced microprocessor chips is extremely low, even though their switching speeds are now quite respectable in comparison to those of the very fastest transistors, and a single chip will now hold a quite complex computer.

While microprocessors do not have the memory bandwidth of supercomputers, the 300-megaflop performance of single-chip processors such as the MIPS 8000 is about one-third the 1-gigaflop performance of each processor in the Cray C-90, a very fast supercomputer. Microprocessor development projects costing hundreds of millions of dollars now produce computing chips with millions of transistors each, and these chips can be sold for a few hundred dollars apiece.

Moreover, because of their greater numbers, software development for small machines proves much more profitable than for large machines. Thus an enormous body of software is available for microprocessor-based computers, whereas only limited software is available for supercomputers.

Parallel Computers: High Performance for Radically Lower Cost

Mass-production economics for hardware and software argue insistently for assembling many microcomputers with their cheap memories into high-performance computers, as an alternative to developing specialized high-performance technology. The idea dates from the 1960s, but the confluence of technical and economic forces for doing so has become much more powerful now than ever before.

CHALLENGES OF PARALLEL COMPUTING

Organizing a coherent simultaneous attack on a single problem by many minds has been a major management challenge for centuries. Organizing a coherent simultaneous attack on a single problem by a large number of processors is similarly difficult. This is the fundamental challenge of parallel computing. It has several aspects.

Applications

It is not evident that every application can be subdivided for a parallel attack. Many believe there are classes of applications that are inherently sequential and can never be parallelized. For example, certain phases in the compilation of a program are by nature sequential processes.

Many applications are naturally parallel. Whenever one wants to solve a problem for a large number of independent input datasets, for example, these can be parceled out among processors very simply. Such problems can be termed intrinsically parallel.

Most applications lie somewhere in between. There are parts that are readily parallelized, and there are parts that seem sequential. The challenge is how to accomplish as much parallelization as is inherently possible. A second challenge of great importance is how to do this *automatically* when one starts with a sequential formulation of the problem solution, perhaps an already existing program.

Hardware Design

How best to connect lots of microprocessors together with each other and with shared resources such as memory and input/output has become a subject of considerable technical exploration and debate. Early attempts to realize the potential performance of parallel processing revealed that too rigid a connection between machines stifles their ability to work by forcing them into lock-step. Too loose a connection makes communication between them cumbersome and slow. The section below, "Parallel Architectures," sketches some of the design approaches that have been pursued.

Numerical Algorithms

During the centuries of hand calculations, people worked one step at a time. Ever since computers were introduced, the programs run on them have been mainly sequential, taking one small step at a time and accomplishing their work rapidly because of the prodigious number of steps that they can take in a short time. The current numerical algorithms for attacking problems are mostly sequential. Even when the mathematics of solution have allowed high degrees of parallel attack, sequential methods have generally been used. In fact, most languages used to express programs, such as FORTRAN, COBOL, and C, enforce sequential organizations on operations that are not inherently sequential.

In the 30 years since parallel computers were conceived, computational scientists have been researching parallel algorithms and rethinking numerical methods for parallel application. This work proceeded slowly, however, because there were few parallel machines from which to benefit if one did come up with a good parallel algorithm, and few on which to develop and test such an algorithm. People didn't work on parallel algorithms because they had no parallel machines to motivate the work; people didn't buy parallel machines because there were few parallel algorithms to make them pay off. The HPCCI and its predecessor initiatives broke this vicious cycle. By funding the development of machines for which little market was developed, and by providing them to computational scientists to use, the HPCCI has vastly multiplied the research efforts on parallel computation algorithms. Nevertheless, 30 years of work on parallel approaches has not yet caught up with four centuries of work on sequential calculation.

Learning New Modes of Thought

Programmers have always been trained to think sequentially. Thinking about numerous steps taken in parallel instead of sequentially may initially seem unnatural. It often requires partitioning a problem in space as well in time. Parallel programming requires new programming languages that can accept suitable statements of the programmer's intent as well as new patterns of thought not yet understood and formalized, much less routinely taught to programmers.

A NEW PARADIGM

By responding to the technological imperative for parallel computing, the HPCCI has in a major way helped add a new paradigm to computing's quiver. Parallel computing is an additional paradigm, not a replacement for sequential and vector computing. Large numbers of researchers have begun to understand the task of harnessing parallel machines and are debating the merits of different parallel architectures. Because the parallel paradigm is new, no one can yet say which particular approaches will prove most successful. It is clear however, that this healthy debate and the workings of the market will identify and develop the best solutions.

Has the parallel computing paradigm really been established as the proper direction for high-performance computing? The Committee to Study High Performance Computing and Communications: Status of a Major Initiative unanimously believes that it has. It is obliged to report, however, that the issue is still being hotly debated in the technical literature. In the November 1994 special issue of the Institute of Electrical and Electronic Engineers *Computer* magazine, Borko Furht asserts in "Parallel Computing: Glory and Collapse" that "the market for massively parallel computers has collapsed, but [academic] researchers are still in love with parallel computing." Furht (1994) argues, "We should stop developing parallel algorithms and languages. We should stop inventing interconnection networks for massively parallel computers. And we should stop teaching courses on advanced parallel programming." An editorial by Lewis (1994) in the same issue similarly discounts highly parallel computing.

Part of the difference of opinion is semantics. Computers have had a few processors working concurrently, at least internal input/output processors, since the late 1950s. Modern vector supercomputers have typically had four or eight processors. The new paradigm concerns *highly* parallel computing, by which some mean hundreds of processors. The committee believes that the number of processors in "parallel" computers in the field will grow normally from a few processors, to a few dozen processors, and thence to hundreds. For the next several years, many computer systems will use moderate parallelism.

The strongest evidence, and that which convinces the committee that the parallel computing paradigm is a long-term trend and not just a bubble, comes from the surging sales of third-generation parallel processors such as the SGI Challenge, the SGI Onyx, and the IBM SP-2. SGI's director of marketing reports, for example, that SGI has sold more than 3,500 Challenge and Onyx machines since September 1993; IBM's Wladawsky-Berger reports that 230 orders for the SP2 have been booked since it was announced in summer 1994 (Parker-Smith, 1994a). In fairness to Furht and Lewis, these surging sales figures have appeared only in the last few months, whereas journal lead times are long.

COMPUTER ARCHITECTURES

Overview

Sequential, Vector

The simple sequential computer fetches and executes instructions from memory one after the other. Each instruction performs a single operation, such as adding, multiplying, or storing one piece of data. Decisions are made by conditionally changing the sequence of instructions depending on the result of some comparison or other operation. Every computer includes memory to store data and results, an instruction unit that fetches and interprets the instructions, and an arithmetic unit that performs the operations (see Figure A.1).

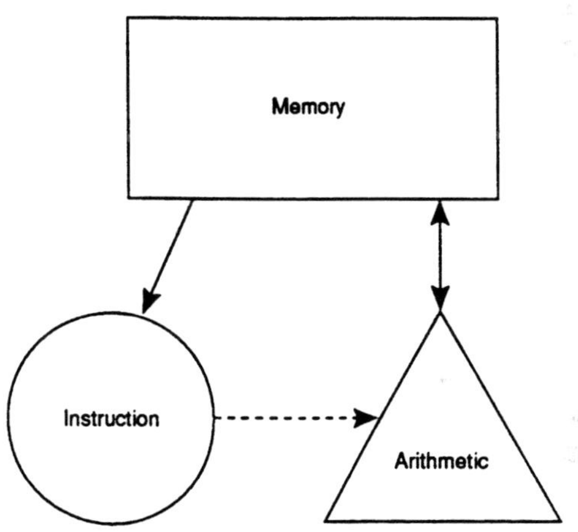

FIGURE A.1 Sequential computer organization.

Vector computers perform the same instruction on each element of a vector or a pair of vectors. A vector is a set of elements of the same type, such as the numbers in a column of a table. So a single "add" operation in a vector computer can cause, for example, one column of 200 numbers to be added, element by element, to another column of 200 numbers. Vector computers can be faster than sequential computers because they do not have to fetch as many instructions to process a given set of data items. Moreover, because the same operation will be done on each element, the flow of vector elements through the arithmetic unit can be pipelined and the operations overlapped on multiple arithmetic units to get higher performance.

Parallel

Parallel computers also have multiple arithmetic units, intended to operate at the same time, or in parallel, rather than in pipelined fashion. Three basic configurations are distinguished according to how many instruction units there are and according to how units communicate with each other. Within each configuration, designs also differ in the patterns, called topologies, for connecting the units to each other to share computational results. Thus applications programmed for a particular computer are not readily portable, even to other computers with the same basic configuration but different topologies.

Single Instruction Multiple Data. In a single instruction multiple data (SIMD) computer, one instruction unit governs the actions of many arithmetic units, each with its own memory. All the arithmetic units march in lock step, obeying the one instruction unit but fetching different operands from their own memories (Figure A.2). Because of the lock step, if any node has to do extra work because of the particular or exceptional values of its data, all the nodes must wait until uniform operations can proceed. Full utilization of all the processor power depends on highly uniform applications.

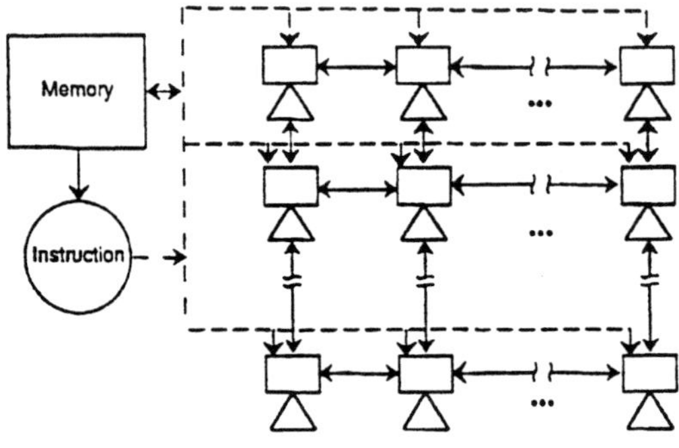

FIGURE A.2 A data-parallel computer organization.

Multiple Instruction Multiple Data Message Passing. In a multiple instruction multiple data (MIMD) message-passing computer, each arithmetic unit has its own memory and its own instruction unit. So each node of such a machine is a complete sequential computer, and each can operate independently. The multiple nodes are connected by communication channels, which may be ordinary computer networks or which may be faster and more efficient paths if all the nodes are in one cabinet. The several nodes coordinate their work on a common problem by passing messages back and forth to each other (Figure A.3). This message-passing takes time and instructions. Various topologies are used to accelerate message routing, which can get complex and take many cycles.

There are two quite different forms of MIMD computers, distinguished by the network interconnecting the processors. One, commonly called a massively parallel processor (MPP), has a collection of processor nodes co-located inside a common cabinet with very high performance specialized interconnections.

The other, often called a workstation farm, consists of a group of workstations connected by conventional local area or even wide area networks. Such collections have demonstrated considerable success on large computing problems that require only modest internode traffic. Between the two extremes of the MPP and the workstation farm lie a number of parallel architectures now being explored. No one can say how this exploration will come out.

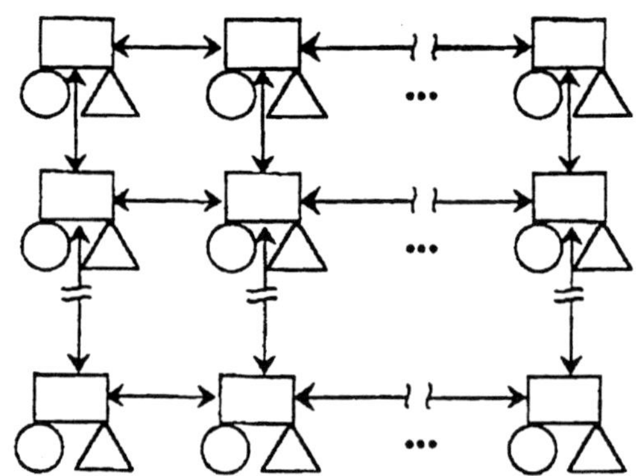

FIGURE A.3 A message-passing parallel computer organization.

Multiple Instruction Multiple Data Shared-Memory. In a multiple instruction multiple data (MIMD) shared-memory computer, the separate nodes share a large common memory. The several nodes coordinate work on a common problem by changing variables in the shared memory, which is a simple and fast operation (Figure A.4).

Each node also has its own memory, generally organized as a *cache* that keeps local copies of things recently accessed from the shared memory. The use of individual cache memories at each processor radically reduces traffic to the shared memory.

The shared memory may be a single physical memory unit, as in the SUN SPARCCenter. This kind of computer organization cannot be scaled indefinitely upward—the shared memory and its bus become a bottleneck at some point.

A more scalable *distributed memory* design has a single shared memory address space, but the physical memory is distributed among the nodes. This arrangement exploits microprocessors' low memory cost and gives better performance for local access. Many experts believe this will become the dominant organization for machines with more than a few processors.

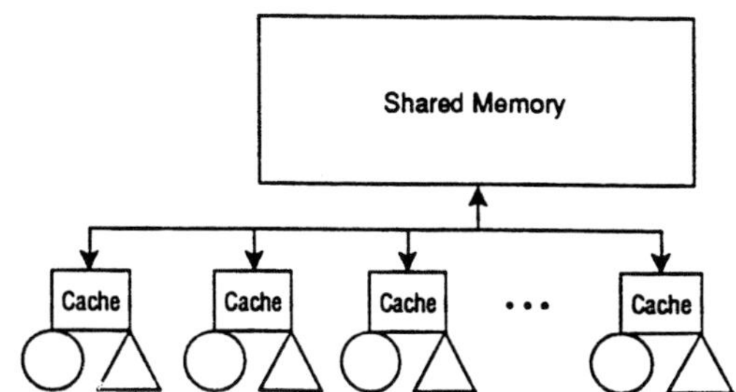

FIGURE A.4 A shared-memory parallel computer organization.

Some distributed-memory machines, such as the Convex Exemplar, enforce cache coherence, so that all processors see the same memory values. Others, such as the Cray T3D, do not enforce coherence but use very fast special circuits to get very low shared-memory latency. Most machines with a shared physical memory maintain cache coherence.

Generations of Parallel Computers

First Commercial Generation: SIMD

Parallel computers with small numbers of processors have been standard commercial fare for 30 years. In some cases, the multiple processors were in duplex, triplex, or quadruplex configurations for high availability; in most advanced computers there have been processors dedicated to input-output. Most vector computers have also been modestly parallel for more than a decade. One-of-a-kind highly parallel computers have been built now and then since the 1960s, with limited success. The Advanced Research Projects Agency (ARPA) recognized the technical-economic imperative to develop highly parallel computers for both military and civilian applications and acted boldly to create its high-performance computing program. This stimulus combined with a ferment of new ideas and with entrepreneurial enthusiasm to encourage several manufacturers to market highly parallel machines, among them Intel, Ncube, Thinking Machines Corporation (TMC), and MasPar. Most of these first-generation machines were SIMD computers, exemplified by the CM1 (Connection Machine 1) developed by Thinking Machines.

Because SIMD execution lacks the information content of multiple instruction flows, applications have to be more uniform to run efficiently on SIMD computers than on other types of parallel computers. Compounding this inherent difficulty, the first-generation machines had only primitive software tools. No application software was available off the shelf, and existing codes could not be automatically ported, so that each application had to be rebuilt from start. Moreover, few of the first-generation machines used off-the-shelf microprocessors with their economic and software advantages.

The first generation of highly parallel computers had some successes but proved to be of too limited applicability to succeed in the general market. Some naturally parallel applications were reprogrammed for these machines, realizing gains in execution speed nearly in proportion to the number of processors applied to the problem, up to tens of processors. The set of applications for which this was true was quite limited, however, and most experts agree that the SIMD configuration has its units too tightly coupled to be used effectively in a wide variety of applications. Nonetheless, the creation of this generation of machines, and their provision of a platform for pioneering and experimental applications, clearly started a great deal of new thinking in academia about how to use such machines.

Second Generation: Message-Passing MIMD

Striving for the wider applicability that would be enabled by a more flexible programming style, parallel computer researchers and vendors developed MIMD configurations made up of complete microprocessors (sometimes augmented by SIMD clusters). By and large, these machines used message-passing for interprocessor communication. The Thinking Machines CM5 is a good example of this second generation. Other examples use off-the-shelf microprocessors as nodes.

Although improving somewhat in ease of use, such machines are still hard to program, and users still need to change radically how they think and the type of algorithms they use. Moreover, because these machines were different both from conventional computers and from first-generation highly parallel computers, the compilers and operating systems again had to be redone "from scratch" and were primitive when the machines were delivered.

The second-generation machines have proven to be much more widely applicable, but primitive operating systems, the continuing lack of off-the-shelf applications, and the difficulties of programming with elementary tools prevented widespread adoption by computer-using industries. As the market registered its displeasure with these inadequacies, several of the vendors of first- and second-generation parallel computers, including TMC and Kendall Square Research, went into Chapter 11 protection or retired from the parallel computer-building field. A beneficial side effect of these collapses has been the scattering of parallel-processing talent to other vendors and users.

As parallel computers gained acceptance, existing vector computer vendors claimed their sales were being harmed by the government promotion and subsidization of a technology that they saw as not yet ready to perform. Cray Research and Convex, among others, saw their sales fall, partly due to performance/cost breakthroughs in smaller computers, partly due to the defense scale-back, and partly due to some customers switching from vector to parallel computers. The complaints of the vector computer vendors triggered studies of the HPCCI by the General Accounting Office and the Congressional Budget Office (see "Concerns Raised in Recent Studies"). Cray Research and Convex have since become important vendors of parallel computers.

Third Generation: Memory-Sharing MIMD

In the third generation, major existing computer manufacturers independently decided that the shared-memory organization, although limited in ultimate scalability, offered the most viable way to meet present market needs. Among others, SGI, Cray Research, and Convex have made such systems using off-the-shelf microprocessors from MIPS, IBM, DEC, and Hewlett-Packard, respectively. As noted above, market acceptance has been encouraging—industrial computer users have been buying the machines and putting them to work. Many users start by using standard software and running the systems as uniprocessors on bread-and-butter jobs, and then expand the utilization of the multiple processors gradually. As parallel algorithms, compilers, languages, and tools continue to develop, these memory-shared machines are well positioned to capitalize on them.

Programming

The development of parallel computing represents a fundamental change not only in the machines themselves, but also in the way they are programmed and used. To use fully the power of a parallel machine, a program must give the machine many independent operations to do simultaneously, and it must organize the communication among the processor nodes. Developing techniques for writing such programs is difficult and is now regarded by the committee as the central challenge of parallel computing.

Computer and computational scientists are now developing new theoretical concepts and underpinnings, new programming languages, new algorithms, and new insights into the application of parallel computing. While much has been done, much remains to be done: even after knowledge about parallel programming is better developed, many existing programs will need to be rewritten for the new systems.

Algorithms

There is a commonly held belief that our ability to solve ever larger and more complex problems is due primarily to hardware improvements. However, A.G. Fraser of AT&T Bell Laboratories has observed that for many important problems the contributions to speed-ups made by algorithmic improvements exceed even the dramatic improvements due to hardware. As a long-term example, Fraser cited the solution of Poisson's equation in three dimensions on a 50 by 50 by 50 grid. This problem, which would have taken years to solve in 1950, will soon be solved in a millisecond. Fraser has pointed out that this speed-up is owing to improvements in both hardware and algorithms, with algorithms dominating.[1]

During the mid-1980s, several scientists independently developed tree codes or hierarchial N-body codes to solve the equations of the gravitational forces for large multibody systems. For 1 million bodies, tree codes are typically 1,000 times faster than classic direct-sum algorithms. More recently, some of these tree-code algorithms have been modified to run on highly parallel computers. For example, Salmon and Warren have achieved a speed-up of 445 times when running their codes on a computer with 512 processors as compared with running them on a single processor (Kaufman and Smarr, 1993, pp. 73-74).

Over the half-century that modern computers have been available, vast improvements in problem solving have been achieved because of new algorithms and new computational models; a short list from among the numerous examples includes:

- Finite-element methods,
- Fast Fourier transforms,
- Monte Carlo simulations,
- Multigrid methods,
- Methods for sparse problems,
- Randomized algorithms,
- Deterministic sampling strategies, and
- Average case analysis.

The exponential increase in the sizes of economical main memories has also enabled a host of new table-driven algorithmic techniques that were unthinkable a decade ago. Discovering and developing new algorithms for solving both generic and specific problems from science, engineering, and the financial services industry, designed and implemented on parallel architectures, will continue to be an important area for national investment.

A SKETCH OF THE HPCCI'S HISTORY

Development and Participants

To quote from the 1993 Blue Book: "The goal of the federal High Performance Computing and Communications Initiative (HPCCI) is to accelerate the development of future generations of high-performance computers and networks and the use of these resources in the federal government and throughout the American economy" (FCCSET, 1992). This goal has grown, like the HPCCI itself, from many roots and has continued to evolve as the initiative has matured. Box A.2 illustrates the evolution of the HPCCI's goals as presented by the Blue Book annual reports.

BOX A.2 HPCCI Goals As Stated in the Blue Books

FY 1992

Accelerate significantly the commercial availability and utilization of the next generation of high-performance computers and networks:

- Extend U.S. technological leadership in high-performance computing and communications.
- Widely disseminate and apply technologies to speed innovation and to serve the national economy, national security, education, and the global environment.
- Spur productivity and competitiveness.

FY 1993

Unchanged.

FY 1994

Goals remained the same with addition of the Information Infrastructure and Technology Applications and program element and mention of the National Information Infrastructure.

FY 1995

Meta-goal ("Accelerate significantly . . . ") not mentioned. Goals consolidated as:

- Extend U.S. technological leadership in high-performance computing and communications; and
- Widely disseminate and apply technologies to speed innovation and to improve national economic competitiveness, national security, education, health care (medicine), and the global environment.

Beginning in the early 1980s, several federal agencies advanced independent programs in high-performance computing and networking.[2] The National Science Foundation (NSF) built on recommendations from the National Science Board Lax report in 1982,[3] as well as a set of internal reports[4] that recommended dramatic action to end the 15-year supercomputer famine in U.S.

universities. NSF asked Congress in 1984 for funds to set up, by a national competition, a number of supercomputer centers to provide academic researchers access to state-of-the-art supercomputers, training, and consulting services. Very quickly this led to the creation of an NSF network backbone to connect the centers. This in turn provided a high-speed backbone for the Internet. Several organizations, including the Office of Management and Budget and the former Federal Coordinating Council on Science, Engineering, and Technology (FCCSET) of the Office of Science and Technology Policy (OSTP), built on these activities and similar efforts in the Department of Energy (DOE),[5] the National Aeronautics and Space Administration (NASA), and the Department of Defense (DOD) to develop the concept of a National Research and Education Network (NREN) program (CSTB, 1988). These explorations were linked to other concurrent efforts to support advanced scientific computing among researchers and to promote related computer and computational science talent development. The result was the High-Performance Computing Program. The program included an emphasis on communications technology development and use from the outset.

High-performance Computing Program structure and strategy were discussed intensively within several federal agencies in 1987-1988, resulting in initial formalization and publication of a program plan in 1989 (OSTP, 1989). OSTP provided a vehicle for interagency coordination of high-performance computing and communications activities, acting through FCCSET and specific subgroups, including the Committee on Physical, Mathematical, and Engineering Sciences; its subordinate Panel on Supercomputers; its High Performance Committee (later subcommittee); its Research Committee (later subcommittee); and its High Performance Computing, Communications, and Information Technology (HPCCIT) Subcommittee. The initial HPCCI effort was concentrated in four agencies: DOD's Advanced Research Projects Agency, DOE, NASA, and NSF. These agencies remain the dominant supporters of computing and computational science research. Although not then a formal member, the National Security Agency (NSA) has also always been an influential player in high-performance computing, due to its cryptography mission needs.

High-performance computing activities received added impetus and more formal status when Congress passed the High-Performance Computing Act of 1991 (PL 102-194) authorizing a 5-year program in high-performance computing and communications. This legislation affirmed the interagency character of the HPCCI, assigning broad research and development (R&D) emphases to the 10 federal agencies that were then participating in the program without precluding the future participation of other agencies. The group of involved agencies expanded to include the Environmental Protection Agency, National Library of Medicine (part of the National Institutes of Health), National Institute of Standards and Technology (part of the Department of Commerce (DOC), and National Oceanographic and Atmospheric Administration (part of DOC) as described in the 1992 and 1993 Blue Books. Additional agencies involved subsequently include the Education Department, NSA, Veterans Administration (now the Department of Veteran Affairs), and Agency for Health Care Policy and Research (part of the Department of Health and Human Services). These and other agencies have participated in HPCCIT meetings and selected projects either as direct members or as observers.

Since its legislative inception in 1991, the HPCCI has attained considerable visibility both within the computer research community and as an important element of the federal government's technology programs. When originally formulated, the HPCCI was aimed at meeting several "Grand Challenges" such as modeling and forecasting severe weather events. It was subsequently broadened to address "National Challenges" relating to several important sectors of the economy, such as manufacturing and health care, and then the improvement of the nation's information infrastructure. The evolution of emphasis on the Grand and National Challenges and also the nation's information infrastructure is outlined in Box A.3.

BOX A.3 From Grand Challenges to the National Information Infrastructure and National Challenges: Evolution of Emphasis as Documented in the Blue Books

FY 1992

- Grand Challenges featured in title and discussed in text
  - Forecasting severe weather events
  - Cancer gene research
  - Predicting new superconductors
  - Simulating and visualizing air pollution
  - Aerospace vehicle design
  - Energy conservation and turbulent combustion
  - Microelectronics design and packaging
  - Earth biosphere research

- National Challenges not discussed

FY 1993

- Grand Challenges featured in title and discussed in text
  - Magnetic recording technology
  - Rational drug design
  - High-speed civil transports (aircraft)
  - Catalysis
  - Fuel combustion
  - Ocean modeling
  - Ozone depletion
  - Digital anatomy
  - Air pollution
  - Design of protein structures
  - Venus imaging
  - Technology links to education

- National Challenges not discussed

FY 1994

- National Information Infrastructure (NII) featured in title
  - Medical emergency and weather emergency discussed as examples of potential use of NII

- Potential National Challenge areas listed in Information Infrastructure Technology and Applications discussion
  - Civil infrastructure
  - Digital libraries
  - Education and lifelong learning
  - Energy management
  - Environment
  - Health care
  - Manufacturing processes and products
  - National security
  - Public access to government information

continues

BOX A.3—*continued*

- Grand Challenges discussed as case studies in text
  - Climate modeling
  - Sharing remote instruments
  - Design and simulation of aerospace vehicles
  - High-performance life science: molecules to magnetic resonance imaging
  - Nonrenewable energy resource recovery
  - Groundwater remediation
  - Improving environmental decision making
  - Galaxy formation
  - Chaos research and applications
  - Virtual reality technology
  - High-performance computing and communications and education
  - Guide to available mathematics software
  - Process simulation and modeling
  - Semiconductor manufacturing for the 21st century
  - Field programmable gate arrays
  - High-performance Fortran and its environment

FY 1995

- National Information Infrastructure featured in title and discussed in text
  - Information infrastructure services
  - Systems development and support environments
  - Intelligent interfaces

- National Challenge areas discussed in text
  - Digital libraries
  - Crisis and emergency management
  - Education and lifelong learning
  - Electronic commerce
  - Energy management
  - Environmental monitoring and waste minimization
  - Health care
  - Manufacturing processes and products
  - Public access to government information

- Major section devoted to "High-Performance Living" with future scenario based on the National Challenges and the National Information Infrastructure

- Grand Challenges discussed in text. More than 30 Grand Challenges illustrated by examples within the following larger areas:
  - Aircraft design
  - Computer science
  - Energy
  - Environmental monitoring and prediction
  - Molecular biology and biomedical imaging
  - Product design and process optimization
  - Space science

Concerns Raised in Recent Studies

A 1993 General Accounting Office (GAO) study of ARPA activities related to the HPCCI and a 1993 Congressional Budget Office (CBO) study of HPCCI efforts in massively parallel computing have been regarded by some as being critical of the entire HPCCI. The committee, which received detailed briefings from the studies' authors, offers the following observations.

GAO Report

The GAO report[6] did not attempt to evaluate the entire HPCCI but focused instead on research funding, computer prototype acquisition activities, and the balance between hardware and software investments by ARPA. It recommended that ARPA (1) broaden its computer placement program by including a wider range of computer types, (2) establish and maintain a public database covering the agency HPCCI program and the performance characteristics of the machines it funds, and (3) emphasize and provide increased support for high-performance software. The report's authors stated to the committee that although recommending improvements, they had found that ARPA had administered its program with propriety.

The committee notes that progress has been made on each of GAO's recommendations, and it has urged that further progress be supported. Committee recommendation 4 calls for further reduction in funding of computer development by vendors and for experimental placement of new machines. These actions should result in a wider variety of machine types as agencies select different machines to meet their mission needs. The National Coordination Office (NCO) has made more program information available and the committee recommends that functions in this area receive added attention by an augmented NCO (recommendation 11). Likewise the committee has called in recommendation 3 for added emphasis on the development of software and algorithms for high-performance computing.

CBO Report

The primary theme of the CBO report (1993) was that because it was aimed primarily at massively parallel machines, which currently occupy only a small part of the computer industry, the High-Performance Computing Systems component of the HPCCI would have little impact on the computer industry. (The high-performance communications and networking segment of the program is not addressed in the CBO report.) The CBO report assumed that the HPCCI was to support the U.S. computer industry, in particular the parallel-computing portion. Although this might be an unstated objective, the explicitly stated goals relate instead to developing new high-performance computer architectures, technologies, and software. The HPCCI appears to be fulfilling the stated goals.

The CBO report did not attempt to analyze the impact of the development of high-performance computing and communications technology on the larger computer industry over a longer period of time. The primary focus of the high-performance computing portion of the program is the creation of scalable parallel machines and software. It is widely believed in both the research and industrial communities that parallelism is a key technology for providing long-term growth in computing performance, as discussed in the early sections of this appendix. The HPCCI has demonstrated a number of successes in academia, in industry, and in government laboratories that provide a significant increase in our ability to build and use parallel machines. Just as reduced instruction set computers (RISC) technology, developed partly with ARPA funding, eventually became a dominant force in computing (some 10 years after the program started), the initiative's ideas are starting to take root in a larger context across the computer industry. Since using parallel processors requires more extensive software changes than did embracing RISC concepts, we should expect that multiprocessor technology will take longer to be adopted.

NOTES

1. A.G. Fraser, AT&T Bell Laboratories, personal communication.

2. Department of Energy (DOE) officials point out that their efforts date from the mid-1970s. For example, in 1974 DOE established a nationwide program providing energy researchers with access to supercomputers and involving a high-performance communications network linking national laboratories, universities, and industrial sites, the precursor of today's Energy Sciences Network (ESNet). See Nelson (1994).

3. *Report of the Panel on Large Scale Computing in Science and Engineering,* Peter Lax, Chairman, sponsored by the U.S. Department of Defense and the National Science Foundation, in cooperation with the Department of Energy and the National Aeronautics and Space Administration, Washington, D.C., December 26, 1982.

4. *A National Computing Environment for Academic Research.* Marcel Bardon and Kent Curtis, NSF Working Group on Computers for Research. National Science Foundation, July 1983.

5. The DOE laboratories had been involved in supercomputing since World War II and were not particularly affected by the setting up of the NSF centers or FCCSET until the late 1980s or early 1990s as the HPCCI emerged.

6. See GAO (1993). Another GAO report (1994) was not released in time for the committee to receive a detailed briefing on which to base further group deliberations. However, observations from that report are drawn in the body of this report.

B
High-Performance Communications Technology and Infrastructure

HIGH-PERFORMANCE COMMUNICATIONS TECHNOLOGY AND INFRASTRUCTURE ADVANCE

The performance/cost imperatives of communications have driven the technology from parallel to serial, from hundreds of slower wires to a few very fast fibers. Fiber-optic transmission offers stunning bandwidths: 100,000 telephone calls or 800 video channels on one pair of fibers. Communications is different from computing. Value often comes from whom one can talk to, rather than how rapidly. Issues of scaling are very important. The scale of the needed networking raises a host of new research issues as to how millions of users can attach to the network.

High-performance computing and high-performance communications support each other in complex ways. Communications has become digital, and the switching of fast digital signals requires high-performance computing technology. On the other hand, very fast computer-to-computer communications are crucial for many applications. Today 16 percent of investment in the High Performance Computing and Communications Initiative (HPCCI) is directed at communications. The communications content of the HPCCI has two aspects: research and development to advance communications and related capabilities (see Table B.1), and delivery of access to communications-based infrastructure to researchers to facilitate their work (see Table B.2). The introduction of the fifth HPCCI component, Information Infrastructure Technology and Applications (IITA), in 1993 appears to extend the second aspect: awards and activities associated with this component appear to emphasize making existing capabilities more useful and more widely used, as opposed to developing new communications-based capabilities, which appears to be largely supported under the National Research and Education Network (NREN) component of the HPCCI.

The Internet is the centerpiece of the present HPCCI communications infrastructure program; it includes the network elements (backbone, regional, and "connections") supported under the NREN program. Thanks to federal support of internetworking technologies that have been applied in the Internet generally and specifically in NREN-supported elements (NSFNET, ESnet, and the NASA Science Internet), the United States has a strong lead in these technologies worldwide. The United States is home to a vital industry that supplies related equipment and software, including businesses begun as spinoffs from academic research activity. See Box B.1 for an example of how government, academic, and industrial investments can complement each other to accelerate the development of a key communications technology.

TABLE B.1 HPCCI Program Activities in Communications Research, FY 1995

Component[a]	Agency[b]	Funding Request for FY 1995 (millions of dollars)	Activity
NREN	ARPA	43.10	Networking
IITA	ARPA	23.00	Global grid communications
BRHR	NSF	11.30	Very high speed networks and optical systems
NREN	NSA	03.50	Very high speed networking
NREN	NSA	02.60	High-speed data protection electronics
NREN	DOE	02.00	Gigabit research and development
NREN	NIST	01.75	Metrology to support mobile and fixed-base communications networks

[a]NREN, National Research and Education Network; IITA, Information Infrastructure Technology and Applications; BRHR, Basic Research and Human Resources.
[b]ARPA, Advanced Research Projects Agency; NSF, National Science Foundation; NSA, National Security Agency; DOE, Department of Energy; NIST, National Institute of Standards and Technology.

TABLE B.2 HPCCI Program Activities in Communications Infrastructure, FY 1995

Component[a]	Agency[b]	Funding Request for FY 1995 (millions of dollars)	Activity[c]
NREN	NSF	46.16	NSFNET
NREN	DOE	14.80	Energy sciences network (ESnet)
NREN		12.70	NREN
NREN	NOAA	08.70	Networking connectivity
NREN	NIH	06.50	NLM medical connections program
NREN	NIST	02.20	NREN deployment and performance measures for gigabit nets and massively parallel processor systems
IITA	NIH	02.00	NCI high-speed networking and distributed conferencing
NREN	EPA	00.70	State network connectivity

[a]NREN, National Research and Education Network; IITA, Information Infrastructure Technology and Applications.
[b]NSF, National Science Foundation; DOE, Department of Energy; NOAA, National Oceanic and Atmospheric Administration; NIH, National Institutes of Health; NIST, National Institute of Standards and Technology; EPA, Environmental Protection Agency.
[c]NLM, National Library of Medicine; NCI, National Cancer Institute.

BOX B.1 Federal Government Participation in the Development of Asynchronous Transfer Mode

The federal government, through the HPCCI and other programs, played a part in the development of the asynchronous transfer mode, or ATM, standard, and most importantly, played a very significant role in developing broad support for ATM as an important switching technology for high-speed computer networks. ATM was developed as a switching technology by the telecommunications community for application in the so-called broadband integrated services digital network, or BISDN. However, its development did not occur without some controversy.

Telecommunications switching had always been based on circuit-switching technologies, which are very well suited to providing fixed-rate connections in a network. Multirate circuit switching can be used to provide connections that are any multiple of some basic rate. Narrowband ISDN is based on these technologies, and most switching and transmission experts in the telecommunications industry expected a straightforward extension of ISDN circuit-switching technology, based on multiples of a 64-Kbps basic rate, into the broadband realm of speeds in the 155-Mbps range.

Variable rate communications services were clearly needed for data communications, as demonstrated by the ARPANET in the 1970s. However, it was also recognized that video and even voice services might be provided in a more efficient manner than was possible through circuit switching if the basic network service could support variable rate communications. Between 1984 and 1987 researchers in leading telecommunications and academic laboratories developed a number of fast-packet switching, or FPS, systems that laid the technological groundwork for the ATM standard. A noted academic researcher participating in this effort was Jonathan Turner, whose work was supported by both NSF and industry funding. Telecommunications industry laboratories such as AT&T, Bellcore, CNET (France), and Bell Telephone Manufacturing (Belgium) also played a significant role. Bellcore, for example, built the first prototype broadband central office in late 1986, and it contained a packet switch that operated at 50 Mbps per line. By 1987, this rate had been extended to nearly 155 Mbps per line. These efforts, in essence, proved that packet switching was capable of running at the data rates required by BISDN. At this time, ARPANET and NSFNET were running at speeds of only 64 Kbps to 1.5 Mbps, and local area networks such as Ethernet ran at speeds of only 10 Mbps.

In late 1986, Gordon Bell, then at NSF, visited Bellcore and received a briefing on fast CMOS-based packet switching technology that had been simulated at speeds of 150 Mbps. Several months later he called a workshop of computer networking researchers to discuss the future of high-speed computer networking. Out of that workshop, from David Farber (University of Pennsylvania) and Bob Kahn (Corporation for National Research Initiatives), came a mid-1987 proposal to NSF to form the gigabit testbed projects.

The telecommunications industry was quite active during this time in developing a standard based on packet switching. In 1988, the Consultative Committee on International Telephony and Telegraphy selected (and named) ATM as the standard for BISDN switching. This action served to focus the telecommunications industry on the development of this technology. However, in 1988 ATM was little more than a name, a basic packet format, and a common cause across the telecommunications industry alone.

In 1989, the gigabit testbed projects were formally initiated with (D)ARPA and NSF funding. One of the objectives of the gigabit testbeds was to determine what switching technologies were appropriate for use in gigabit networking. There were several major contenders: ATM, HiPPi (a switching technology favored by the supercomputer community), and PTM (a proprietary packet-switching technology advocated by IBM, different from ATM primarily in that it used variable-sized packets). Although it would be several years before conclusive results from the testbeds were produced, the use of ATM in the testbeds gave it wide exposure within the federal government's technology community.

continues

BOX B.1—*continued*

In 1990, the first company devoted solely to producting ATM products was formed. The founders of FORE Systems were first exposed to ATM technology through their participation in the NECTAR gigabit testbed. Cross-testbed exchanges were encouraged by the gigabit testbed program, and in 1989 and 1990 there were meetings of the Bellcore and MIT researchers working on ATM for Aurora and the Carnegie Mellon University researchers working on NECTAR. FORE was founded in 1990 and subsisted through its first product development cycle largely on research and prototyping contracts from ARPA and the Naval Research Laboratory. FORE's first products were delivered to the Naval Research Laboratory in 1991. FORE today is a rapidly growing company with nearly 300 employees and one of the leading manufacturers of ATM switching equipment.

In 1990, a collaboration was formed between Apple, Bellcore, Sun Microsystems, and Xerox to attempt to gain the acceptance of ATM as a new local area networking standard. This group, which eventually expanded to include Digital and Hewlett-Packard, produced the first published specification of ATM for Local Networking Applications in April 1991. ARPA participated in informal discussions with this group via its ARPA Networking Principal Investigator meetings, looking for opportunities to fund technical work that would be necessary to make ATM useful for local area networking. One notable result of ARPA's funding was the first implementation of the Q.2931 ATM signaling standard, which was required to allow ATM to implement switched (as opposed to permanent) virtual circuits. Another result was the implementation, by Xerox, of an ATM switch architecture that is well suited for low-cost implementation. This work, funded in part by ARPA, served to accelerate the development of an industry standard for local ATM by the ATM Forum.

Once ATM had been established as both a computer and telecommunications networking standard, the role of the federal government turned toward developing an early market for high-speed networking equipment and services. Several notable programs greatly expanded this early market. One has been the gigabit testbeds. Some of the first installations of 2.4-Gbps SONET and ATM by several telecommunications carriers were for these testbeds. Although the federal government did not spend a single dollar for these facilities, its leadership of the gigabit testbed program was critical in getting telecommunications carriers to construct these very expensive facilities for the testbeds. Telecommunications equipment manufacturers benefited directly and saw their development of very high speed (full-duplex 622-Mbps) ATM equipment greatly accelerated.

Some direct federal procurements of ATM and SONET services are still playing a key role in the development of the marketplace. An important procurement of ATM and SONET services and technology was the Washington Area Bitway (WABitway), the first significant sale of high-speed SONET services by Bell Atlantic. In early 1994, NSF announced the selection of a number of companies to provide ATM-based communications services for the new NSFNET. Telecommunications companies involved in this project include Ameritech, MCI, MFS Datanet, Pacific Bell, and Sprint.

Eight HPCCI program activities are directed primarily at communications infrastructure, principally supporting deployment of the Internet within each agency's community. Several of the infrastructure programs are building on early results of the gigabit testbed research. For example, ATM and SONET networking technologies, first deployed in the gigabit testbeds in 1992, appear in some form in many of the FY 1995 infrastructure activities.

Developing and broadening access to information infrastructure pose many research issues. Information infrastructure is more complex than networks, per se, and the computing and communications research community has already helped to explore and define fundamental concepts, for example, the concept of "middleware" to cover the kind of internal services that help to transform a network into information infrastructure. Research into how to implement such services has begun under the HPCCI umbrella. More specifically, the National Aeronautics and Space Administration, the National Science Foundation, and the Advanced Research Projects Agency have combined to fund research to support the development of digital libraries, providing a vehicle for exploring many concepts associated with information infrastructure (NSF, 1993).

The concept of a better nationwide information infrastructure, itself connected to a global information infrastructure, poses yet other concerns associated with interconnecting multiple kinds of networks from multiple kinds of providers to multiple kinds of users offering multiple kinds of services. This construct adds great complexity, increasing the emphasis on scale and architecture and adding in such concerns as heterogeneity of systems, decentralization of control and management, routing, security, and so on. There have been many government, academic, and industry studies under way to identify and clarify these research issues. Although the newspapers are filled with announcements of corporate alliances, new venture formations, and new product introductions more or less linked to the advancement of the nation's information infrastructure, significant advances call for the solution of many technical problems and therefore for a significant research effort.

C
Review of the High Performance Computing and Communications Initiative Budget

The committee attempted a nontraditional look at how High Performance Computing and Communications Initiative (HPCCI) funds are being invested.[1] Traditional HPCCI budget reports show budget breakdowns by agency and by program component (High-Performance Computing Systems, National Research and Education Network, Advanced Software Technology and Algorithms, Information Infrastructure Technology and Applications, and Basic Research and Human Resources). The committee found it informative to examine the funding from a functional perspective to understand what sort of technical work is being performed and in what quantity.

The committee separated the 88 HPCCI program elements into 11 disciplines defined as indicated below:

- *Computer technology (CPT)*—applied research directed at advancing the state of computer architecture and hardware technology;

- *Software technology (SWT)*—applied research directed at advancing the state of computer software technology;

- *Communications technology (CMT)*—applied research directed at advancing the state of communications technology;

- *Computing infrastructure (CPI)*—acquisition and operation of supercomputer facilities;

- *Communications infrastructure (CMI)*—acquisition and operation of high-performance computer communications networks and services;

- *Applications and computational science (APP)*—creation of software and computational techniques directed at solving specific scientific problems and applications;

- *Common applications support (CAS)*—creation of software and computational techniques to support a range of applications across multiple disciplines;

- *Artificial intelligence and human-machine interaction (AI)*—applied research directed at solving artificial intelligence and human interface problems.

• *Basic hardware technology (BHW)*—basic electronics research supporting electronic components that might be applied to a wide variety of systems, including computers and communications systems;

• *Education (EDU)*—training and education; and

• *Administration (ADM)*—National Coordination Office.

The committee classified 86 of the 88 program elements as coming under 1 of the 11 disciplines listed above, based on each program element's FY 1995 milestones (Table C.1). If a program element appeared to fit into more than one discipline, the committee categorized it by examining the element's milestones to determine where the majority of the program activity was concentrated. Two of the larger Advanced Research Projects Agency (ARPA) program activities (Intelligent Systems and Software, and Information Sciences) were split between two disciplines.

Table C.2 shows the FY 1993 actual budget, the FY 1995 request,[2] and the percentage change in the HPCCI budget for each of these 11 disciplines.

BUDGET REVIEW

It is interesting to examine the HPCCI budget to see which areas are being emphasized and to compare these with the HPCCI's goals and objectives. As indicated also in Chapter 2, the current program goals are as follows:

• Extend U.S. leadership in high-performance computing and networking technologies;
• Disseminate the technologies to accelerate innovation and serve the economy, national security, education, and the environment; and
• Spur gains in U.S. productivity and industrial competitiveness.

The computer technology, software technology, and communications technology disciplines address the goals of extending technical leadership in computing and communications and providing key enabling technologies for the information infrastructure. The budget for these three disciplines accounted for 32.9 percent of the FY 1993 actual budget and 30.5 percent of the FY 1995 requested budget.

The largest part of the HPCCI budget is invested in applications and supercomputer computing infrastructure to support applications—49.8 percent of the FY 1993 actual budget and 50.1 percent of the FY 1995 requested budget. Applications and computational science, common applications support, artificial intelligence and human-machine interaction, and computing infrastructure programs are included. The rest of the budget requested for FY 1995 is divided among basic hardware technology (5.1 percent), communications infrastructure (7.9 percent), education (5.6 percent), and a very small amount for program administration.

TABLE C.1 Mapping of Agencies, HPCCI Budget Allocations, Program Elements, and Discipline Categories

Agency[a]	1995 Requested ($M)	1993 Actual ($M)	Discipline[b]	Program Element[c]
ARPA	36.15	11.35	AI	Intelligent systems and software
ARPA	36.15	11.35	SWT	
ARPA	60.20	44.90	CPT	Scalable computing systems
ARPA	44.50	33.50	BHW	Microsystems
ARPA	43.10	34.80	CMT	Networking
ARPA	33.90	38.00	SWT	National-scale information enterprises
ARPA	29.60	36.50	SWT	Scalable software
ARPA	23.00	00.00	CMT	Global grid communications
ARPA	10.50	15.10	AI	Information sciences
ARPA	10.50	15.10	SWT	
ARPA	14.00	13.90	EDU	Foundations
ARPA	09.80	00.00	APP	Health information infrastructure
ARPA	06.00	00.00	BHW	Integrated command and control technology
NSF	76.43	63.89	CPI	Supercomputer centers
NSF	46.16	30.10	CMI	NSFNET
NSF	35.25	00.00	CAS	Information infrastructure technology and applications program
NSF	25.35	21.79	SWT	Software systems and algorithms
NSF	20.95	18.65	CPI	Research infrastructure
NSF	20.70	18.76	CPT	Computing systems and components
NSF	20.24	15.34	EDU	Education and training
NSF	11.50	07.80	APP	Biological sciences (non-NC/GC)
NSF	11.30	09.80	CMT	Very high speed networks and optical systems
NSF	11.00	10.40	AI	Human machine interaction and information access
NSF	10.75	07.00	CAS	Grand Challenge applications groups
NSF	10.55	09.20	CAS	Research centers
NSF	09.77	02.75	APP	Physical sciences (non-NC/GC)
NSF	07.59	05.72	CAS	Computational mathematics (non-NC/GC)

continues

TABLE C.1—*continued*

Agency[a]	1995 Requested ($M)	1993 Actual ($M)	Discipline[b]	Program Elements[c]
NSF	04.23	02.17	APP	Engineering (non-NC/GC)
NSF	03.84	01.15	CPI	Geosciences (non-NC/GC)
NSF	03.01	00.65	APP	Social, behavioral, and economic sciences (non-NC/GC)
DOE	35.60	35.13	CPI	Supercomputer access
DOE	16.00	15.25	CAS	Basic research for applied mathematics research
DOE	14.80	07.68	CMI	Energy sciences network (ESnet)
DOE	12.90	07.15	CPI	High-performance computing research centers
DOE	12.60	08.98	CAS	Software components and tools
DOE	09.90	07.73	CPI	Evaluation of early systems
DOE	09.00	06.53	APP	Enabling energy Grand Challenges
DOE	03.40	02.44	CAS	Computational techniques
DOE	03.00	02.36	EDU	Education, training, and curriculum
DOE	02.00	02.60	EDU	Research participation and training
DOE	02.00	01.86	CMT	Gigabit research and development
DOE	02.00	01.80	APP	High-performance research centers—global climate collaboration
DOE	01.20	00.00	CAS	Information infraservices
DOE	01.00	00.00	CPI	Advanced prototype systems
NASA	55.30	46.80	APP	Grand Challenge support
NASA	26.40	17.60	CPI	Testbeds
NASA	12.70	08.50	CMI	National Research and Education Network (NREN)
NASA	10.70	00.00	EDU	Information infrastructure applications
NASA	09.20	05.40	SWT	Systems software
NASA	06.80	00.00	CAS	Information infrastructure technology
NASA	03.80	03.30	EDU	Basic research and human resources
NIH	11.00	08.00	CPI	DCRT high-performance biomedical computing program

continues

TABLE C.1—*continued*

Agency[a]	1995 Request ($M)	1993 Actual ($M)	Discipline[b]	Program[c]
NIH	11.00	01.50	APP	National Library of Medicine high-performance computing and communications health care applications
NIH	08.80	03.40	APP	NCRR information infrastructure technology applications
NIH	08.80	06.80	APP	NCRR advanced software technology and algorithms
NIH	06.70	06.30	CPI	NCI Frederick biomedical supercomputing center
NIH	06.50	00.40	CMI	NLM medical connections program
NIH	05.40	03.80	CAS	NLM IAIMS grants
NIH	05.00	03.10	EDU	NCRR basic research and human resources
NIH	04.80	04.10	APP	NLM biotechnology informatics
NIH	04.70	05.00	CAS	NLM intelligent agent database searching
NIH	03.60	02.90	EDU	NLM HPCCI training grants
NIH	02.20	01.50	APP	NLM electronic imaging
NIH	02.00	00.00	CMI	NCI high-speed networking and distributed conferencing
NIH	00.70	00.40	ADM	National Coordination Office
NIH	00.60	00.00	APP	High-performance communications for PDQ, Cancer Net, and electronic publishing
NSA	26.10	00.00	CPT	Supercomputing research
NSA	05.70	00.00	SWT	Secure operating system development
NSA	03.50	00.00	CMT	Very high speed networking
NSA	02.60	00.00	CMT	High-speed data protection electronics
NSA	02.00	00.00	BHW	Superconducting research
NSA	00.23	00.00	EDU	Technology-based training
NIST	25.20	00.00	CAS	Systems integral for manufacturing applications
NIST	07.60	00.60	APP	Development and dissemination of scientific software for high-performance computing systems

continues

TABLE C.1—*continued*

Agency[a]	1995 Requested ($M)	1993 Actual ($M)	Discipline[b]	Program Element[c]
NIST	06.45	00.00	BHW	Metrology for future generations of microelectronics
NIST	04.00	00.00	CAS	Language, image, and text processing
NIST	04.00	00.00	SWT	Specification and testing of high-integrity, distributed systems
NIST	02.75	00.00	CAS	Support for electronic commerce
NIST	02.20	01.50	CMT	Deployment and performance measures for gigabit nets and massively parallel processor systems
NIST	01.75	00.00	CMT	Metrology to support mobile and fixed-base communications networks
NIST	01.25	00.00	CAS	Electronic libraries and distributed multimedia applications
NIST	01.20	00.00	SWT	Assurance, reliability, and integrity of NREN objects
NOAA	16.05	09.40	APP	Advanced computation
NOAA	08.70	00.40	CMI	Networking connectivity
NOAA	00.50	00.00	APP	Information dissemination pilots
EPA	06.45	05.33	APP	Environmental modeling
EPA	05.25	01.31	APP	Computational techniques
EPA	01.97	01.16	EDU	Education and training
EPA	00.70	00.21	CMI	State network connectivity
EPA	00.30	00.00	APP	Public data access

[a]ARPA, Advanced Research Projects Agency; NSF, National Science Foundation; DOE, Department of Energy; NASA, National Aeronautics and Space Administration; NIH, National Institutes of Health; NSA, National Security Agency; NIST, National Institute of Standards and Technology; NOAA, National Oceanographic and Atmospheric Administration; EPA, Environmental Protection Agency.

[b]AI, artificial intelligence and human-machine interaction; SWT, software technology; CPT, computer technology; BHW, basic hardware technology; CMT, communications technology; EDU, education and training; APP, applications and computational science; CAS, common applications support; CPI, computing infrastructure; CMI, communications infrastructure; ADM, National Coordination Office.

[c]NC/GC, National Challenge/Grand Challenge; DCRT, Division of Computer Research and Technology (NIH); IAIMS, Integrated Academic Information Management System; NLM, National Library of Medicine; NCRR, National Center for Research Resources (NIH); NCI, National Cancer Institute (NIH); PDQ, Physician Data Query (NIH).

SOURCE: Data on agency budgets and program activities were extracted from the *FY 1995 Implementation Plan* prepared by the National Coordination Office (1994).

TABLE C.2 Actual FY 1993 and Requested FY 1995 HPCCI Budget (millions of dollars) Categorized by Discipline

Discipline	1993	1995	Percentage Change
Computer technology	63.66	107.00	68
Software technology	128.14	155.60	21
Communications technology	47.96	89.45	86
Computing infrastructure	165.60	204.72	23
Communications infrastructure	47.29	91.56	94
Applications and computational science	102.44	176.96	73
Common applications support	57.39	147.44	157
Artificial intelligence and human-machine interaction	36.85	57.65	56
Basic hardware technology	33.50	58.95	76
Education	44.66	64.54	45
Administration	0.40	0.70	75
TOTAL program	727.89	1154.56	59

Alternatively, the 11 discipline categories can be used to examine the balance between support for discipline-specific scientific research that uses high-performance computing and communications technologies and support for computer science research on new high-performance computing and communications technologies. Analysis of the FY 1995 HPCCI budget request shows that $352 million (30 percent) would be invested in basic research in computer, software, and communications technologies; $205 million (18 percent) in applied computer science research, artificial intelligence, and human-machine interaction; $176 million (15 percent) in direct support of applications and computational science; and $297 million (26 percent) in computing and communications infrastructure.

Commentary: Many Possibilities for Misinterpretation

The HPCCI has enjoyed a certain amount of political support and is growing even in a time of very tight federal budgets. The committee believes that this has created a "bandwagon" effect: the initiative has had its scope extended by the inclusion of some work not directly related to the HPCCI's goals, however valuable it may be, or work with broad relevance. The result has been a less than focused program.

For example, all high-performance computing and communications systems are built from electronics and depend directly on advancements in basic electronic technology. The ARPA Microsystems program activity, which constitutes the large majority of the basic hardware discipline, supports research in basic electronics technologies. This research will eventually benefit the high-performance computing and communications technology base and help advance the nation's information infrastructure, but it could also be used in a wide variety of other contexts.

Another problem is the possible creation of false expectations about the extent to which the HPCCI could create the technology necessary for advancing the nation's information infrastructure. A large amount of work within the two applications disciplines is directed primarily toward the use of high-performance computing in solving certain scientific and agency mission problems. Only a part of this work, such as the creation of digital libraries, would apply directly to the goal of enhancing the nation's information infrastructure. Some of this work is directed at challenging computational science problems, which have excellent scientific impact but whose results are more easily justified as scientific results, rather than HPCCI results. Also, the HPCCI invests much more heavily in computing than in communications. Less than 16 percent of the FY 1995 request is for communications technology and infrastructure.

About one-third of the program is directed toward creating new technology directly applicable to advancing the information infrastructure. The growth in funding in these areas is offset by an unrelated decrease in research investment by industry, spurred in part by competitive changes in the computer and communications industries. As a result, the nation's total amount of research in high-performance computing and communications technologies is considerably less than it appears, and in fact may be insufficient to maintain the strategic U.S. lead in these technologies or to support the rapid deployment of an enhanced information infrastructure.

NOTES

1. CPSMA (1994), p. 7; this report points out that labor-intensive, detailed disaggregation of published data may be the only way to understand how research program budgets are spent.

2. Amounts shown for FY 1995 are Executive Budget requests. At press time, agency appropriations had been made, but the involved agencies had not disaggregated the appropriations and reported the HPCCI portions to the National Coordination Office. A 2-year time period, FY 1993 to FY 1995, was used to help dampen any single-year jumps in level.

D
Current High Performance Computing and Communications Initiative Grand Challenge Activities

Since its beginning, the High Performance Computing and Communications Initiative has included Grand Challenges, difficult scientific problems whose solution will yield new scientific understanding while simultaneously advancing high-performance computing and communications. The following list of current Grand Challenge activities is based on the FY 1994 and FY 1995 "Blue Books" and communications with National Coordination Office staff.

NATIONAL SCIENCE FOUNDATION

Aerospace

- Coupled field problems

Computer Science

- Machine learning
- Parallel input/output (I/O) methods for I/O-intensive Grand Challenges

Environmental Modeling and Prediction

- Large-scale environmental modeling
- Adaptive coordination of results of predictive models with experimental observations
- Earthquake ground motion modeling in large basins
- High-performance computing for land cover dynamics
- Massively parallel simulation of large-scale, high-resolution ecosystem models

Molecular Biology and Biomedical Imaging

- Biomolecular design
- Imaging in biological research
- Advanced computational approaches to biomolecular modeling and structure determination
- Understanding human joint mechanics through advanced computational models

Product Design and Process Optimization

- High-capacity atomic-level simulations for the design of materials

Space Science

- Black hole binaries: coalescence and gravitational radiation
- Formation of galaxies and large-scale structure
- Radio synthesis imaging

DEPARTMENT OF ENERGY

Energy

- Mathematical combustion modeling
- Quantum chromodynamics calculations
- Oil reservoir modeling
- Numerical Tokamak project

Environmental Monitoring and Prediction

- Computational chemistry (see Box D.1 for discussion)
- Global climate modeling
- Groundwater transport and remediation

Molecular Biology and Biomedical Imaging

- Computational structural biology

Product Design and Process Optimization

- First-principles simulation of materials properties

NATIONAL AERONAUTICS AND SPACE ADMINISTRATION

- Large-scale structure and galaxy formation
- Cosmology and accretion astrophysics
- Convective turbulence and mixing in astrophysics
- Solar activity and heliospheric dynamics

NATIONAL INSTITUTES OF HEALTH

- Molecular biology
- Biomedical imaging

NATIONAL INSTITUTE OF STANDARDS AND TECHNOLOGY

- Product design and process optimization

ENVIRONMENTAL PROTECTION ADMINISTRATION

- Linked air and water-quality modeling

NATIONAL OCEANIC AND ATMOSPHERIC ADMINISTRATION

- Climate change prediction and weather forecasting

BOX D.1 Computational Chemistry: Applying High-Performance Computing to Scientific Problems

Chemists were among the earliest researchers to pursue the use of computers to extend understanding of their field. At the time of a 1956 Texas conference on quantum chemistry, electronic computers had developed to the stage that it was just feasible to program large scientific computations. However, these computers provided results too crude to be of interest to quantum chemists, even by the late 1960s. Nonetheless, based on this "progress," the conference passed a recommendation urging that more machines be at the disposal of university departments. Several groups at the University of Chicago, the Massachusetts Institute of Technology, and elsewhere pursued the goal of exploiting these new facilities, engaging in huge (for the time) research programs to compute the electronic wave functions for molecules constituted of two atoms from the first full row of the periodic chart.

By the early 1970s, significant progress had been made in the computation of molecular energies, wave functions, and dynamics of reacting systems and liquid structure by high-speed computers of the day, namely, the IBM 360/65, CDC 6600, and Univac 1108. Important work was also being done using semiempirical methods for systems with as many as 10 to 12 atoms. Reliable methods had been applied to the calculation of potential energy surfaces for $H + H_2$ and $F + H_2$ systems—methods that have been essential in the advancement of understanding molecular collisions. There had been semi-quantitative calculations of hydrogen bond strengths and protein conformation, but the facilities to carry out such work were available to only a small group of chemists, mostly on the staffs of national laboratories. The need to extend access to such facilities coupled with the new goal of bringing together people to work on software development and to attack important problems in chemistry led to the creation of the National Resource for Computation in Chemistry (NRCC) funded jointly by the National Science Foundation (NSF) and Department of Energy.

With the creation of the NSF supercomputer centers in the 1980s, chemists were able to pursue computational studies with requirements well beyond the capability of systems available otherwise even to leading research groups of the period. In addition to high-speed computation, the centers made accessible large amounts of disk storage and fostered large-scale use of high-speed data communication.

A major breakthrough of the early 1980s was the recognition by industry of the value of computational chemistry to the marketplace. Companies set up research groups that used computational chemistry software for electronic structure studies (e.g., Gaussian and CADPAC) and molecular mechanics simulations (e.g., AMBER and CHARMM), coupled with graphics platforms.

By the mid-1980s an industry had developed in modeling software focused on the chemical, pharmaceutical, and biotechnology industries. Large companies, such as Eli Lilly and Dupont, bought supercomputers to provide the capability to model complex molecules and processes important for their businesses.

One of the major directions for future work is the application of accurate quantum mechanical approaches to biological systems. This effort would complement the molecular mechanics method with selected calculations of higher accuracy to enable explication of important fine points. Areas where these efforts might be introduced are enzymatic reactions involving transition-metal centers and an array of catalytic processes.

The additional power provided by massively parallel computer systems is stimulating a push for higher accuracy and improved algorithms. Methods that have had impact for serial processors that were readily modified for vector systems often must undergo major modification or replacement for massively parallel processors. A major requirement for advancement is seamless scalability across systems of different size.

With the need for higher accuracy on massively parallel systems will likely come increased attention to Monte Carlo methods for quantum many-body systems. Quantum simulations are naturally parallel and are expected to be used increasingly on massively parallel computer systems.

E
Accomplishments of National Science Foundation Supercomputer Centers

INTRODUCTION

The National Science Foundation (NSF) Supercomputer Centers Program preceded the High Performance Computing and Communications Initiative but has become an integral and important part of it. The centers were established to provide access to high-performance computing—supercomputers and related resources—for the broad science and engineering research community. The program has evolved from one comprising independent, competitive, and duplicative computer centers to a cooperative activity, one that has been characterized as a MetaCenter.

In 1992 the four NSF supercomputer centers (Cornell Theory Center, National Center for Supercomputing Applications, Pittsburgh Supercomputer Center, and San Diego Supercomputer Center) formed a collaboration based on the concept of a national MetaCenter for computational science and engineering: a collection of intellectual and physical resources unlimited by geographical or institutional constraints. The centers' first mission was to provide a stable source of computer cycles for a large community of scientists and engineers. The primary objective was to help researchers throughout the country make effective use of the architecture or combination of architectures best suited to their work. Another objective was to educate and train students and researchers from academia and industry to use and test the limits of supercomputing in solving complex research problems. The best and most adventurous proposals for using an expensive and limited resource were sought.

In 1994, the scientific computing division of the National Center for Atmospheric Research joined the MetaCenter. In addition, the NSF established the MetaCenter Regional Affiliates program, under which other institutions could pursue projects of interest in collaboration with MetaCenter institutions. The MetaCenter thus became a unique resource and a laboratory for computer scientists and computational scientists working together on shared tasks.

IMPORTANT TECHNOLOGY ACCOMPLISHMENTS

Originally set up in 1985 to provide national access to traditional supercomputers, the NSF centers have evolved to a much larger mission. The centers now offer a wide variety of high-performance architectures from a large array of U.S. vendors. Today work at the centers is dominated by research efforts in software, in collaboration with computer scientists, focusing on operating systems, compilers, network control, mathematical libraries, and programming languages and environments.

Supercomputer Usage at NSF Centers

Table E.1 shows the growth in the number of users and in the availability of cycles at the NSF supercomputer centers from 1986 to 1994. See also Figure E.1. The increase in capacity in 1993 was owing mainly to the introduction of new computing architectures. The slight decrease in the number of users reflects the centers' effort to encourage users able to meet their computational needs with the increasingly powerful workstations of the mid-1990s to use their own institutional resources.

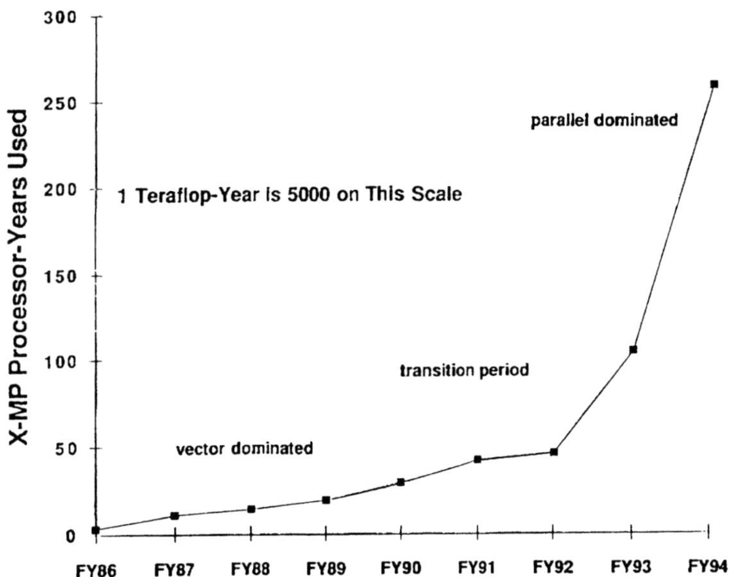

FIGURE E.1 Total historical usage of all high-performance computers in the NSF MetaCenter. This graph shows the total annual usage of all high-performance computers in MetaCenter facilities. Particularly striking is the growth since 1992, when microprocessors in various parallel configurations began to be employed. All usage has been converted to equivalent processor-years for a Cray Research Y-MP, the type of supercomputer that the NSF centers first installed in 1985-1986.

TABLE E.1 Supercomputer Usage at National Science Foundation Supercomputer Centers, 1986 to 1994

Fiscal Year	Active Users	Usage in Normalized CPU Hours[a]
1986	1,358	29,485
1987	3,326	95,752
1988	5,069	121,615
1989	5,975	165,950
1990	7,364	250,628
1991	7,887	361,037
1992	8,578	398,932
1993	7,730	910,088
1994	7,431	2,249,562

[a]Data prior to May 1990 include the John von Neumann Center.

Architectures and Vendors

The national research community has been offered access to a wide and continually updated set of high-performance architectures since the beginning of the NSF Supercomputer Centers Program in 1985. The types of architectures and number of vendors are now probably near an all-time high (Table E.2), allowing the science and engineering communities maximum choice in selecting a machine that matches their computational needs. A short list of architectures offered through the NSF centers program includes single and clustered high-performance workstations or workstation multiprocessors, minicomputers, graphics supercomputers, mainframes with or without attached processors or vector units, vector supercomputers, and single instruction multiple data (SIMD) and multiple instruction multiple data (MIMD) massively parallel processors.

TABLE E.2 Vector and Scalable Parallel High-Performance Computing Machines in the Four National Science Foundation Supercomputer Centers

FY 1991 7 Vector supercomputers
2 IBM 3090—6 processors each (new)
2 Cray YMP—8 processors each
Cray YMP—4 processors
Cray 2S—4 processors
Convex C240—4 processors
FY 1991 4 Scalable parallel systems
2 TMC CM2—32,000 processors each
Intel iPSC/860—32 processors (new)
Alliant 2800—14 processors (new)
FY 1992 6 Vector supercomputers
IBM ES9000/900—6 processors (upgrade)
2 Cray YMP—8 processors each
Cray YMP—4 processors
Cray 2S—4 processors
Convex C3880—8 processors (upgrade)
FY 1992 11 Scalable parallel systems
2 TMC CM2—32,000 processors each
TMC CM5—512 processors
Intel iPSC/860—64 processors
nCUBE2—128 processors (new)
Kendall Square Research, KSR1—64 processors (new)
IBM PVS—32 processors (new)
Alliant 2800—14 processors
2 DEC Workstation Cluster (new)
IBM Workstation Cluster (new)

continues

TABLE E.2—*continued*

FY 1993 Vector supercomputers
IBM ES9000/900—6 processors Cray C90—16 processors (upgrade) Cray YMP—8 processors Cray YMP—4 processors Cray 2S—4 processors Convex C3880—8 processors
FY 1993 14 Scalable parallel systems
2 TMC CM2—32,000 processors each TMC CM5—512 processors Intel Paragon—400 processors (upgrade) nCUBE2—128 processors KSR1—160 processors (upgrade) IBM PVS—32 processors IBM SP1—64 processors (new) Cray T3D—32 processors (new) 2 DEC Workstation Cluster IBM Workstation Cluster HP Workstation Cluster (new) MasPar 2—16,000 processors (new)
FY 1994 5 Vector supercomputers
IBM ES9000/900—6 processors Cray C90—16 processors Cray C90—8 processors (upgrade) Cray YMP—4 processors Convex C3880—8 processors
FY 1994 18 Scalable parallel systems
TMC CM2—32,000 processors TMC CM2—8,000 processors TMC CM5—512 processors Intel Paragon—400 processors (upgrade) Intel Paragon—28 processors (new) nCUBE2—128 processors KSR1—128 processors IBM PVS—32 processors IBM SP1—64 processors IBM SP2—80 processors (new) Cray T3D—512 processors 2 DEC Workstation Cluster IBM Workstation Cluster HP Workstation Cluster MasPar 2—16,000 processors Convex Exemplar—8 processors (new) SGI Challenge—32 processors (new)

Current vendors whose top machines have been made available include IBM, DEC, Hewlett-Packard, Silicon Graphics Inc., Sun Microsystems, Cray Research, Convex Computer, Intel Supercomputer, Thinking Machines Corporation, and nCUBE, plus a number of companies no longer in existence, such as Alliant, Floating Point Systems, ETA, Kendall Square Research, Stellar, Ardent, and Stardent.

Access and New Architectures

In the 1960s, only a few universities had access to state-of-the-art supercomputers. By the early 1990s, some 15,000 researchers in over 200 universities had used one or more of the supercomputers in the NSF MetaCenter. This increased use led to new concepts and innovation:

- *Achieving production parallelism.* Cornell Theory Center became the first member center to achieve production parallelism on a vector supercomputer.

- *Migration to the UNIX operating system.* In 1987, the National Center for Supercomputing Applications (NCSA) became the first major supercomputer center to migrate its Cray supercomputer from CTSS to UNICOS, a UNIX-based operating system developed at Cray Research for its supercomputers.

- *Access to massively parallel computers.* NCSA introduced massively parallel computing (MPP) to the research community with the CM-2 in 1989, followed by the CM-5 in 1991. NCSA has worked closely with national users and the computer science community to create a wide range of 512-way parallel application codes that can in 1995 be moved to other large MPP architectures such as the T3D at PSC, the Intel Paragon at SDSC, or the IBM SP-2 at CTC.

- *Heterogeneous processors.* In 1991, the Pittsburgh Supercomputer Center was the first site to distribute code between a massively parallel machine (TMC-CM2) and a vector supercomputer (Cray Y-MP), linked by a high-speed channel (HiPPI).

- *Workstation clusters.* The NSF supercomputer centers were among the first to experiment with clusters of workstations as an alternative for scalable computing. The first work was done in the 1980s with loosely coupled clusters of Silicon Graphics Inc. workstations to create frames for scientific visualizations. With the introduction of the IBM RS6000, several centers moved to study tightly coupled networks and developed job control software. Clusters from DEC, Hewlett-Packard, and Sun Microsystems are now available as well.

Storage Technologies, File Format, and File Systems

With the vast increase in both simulation and observational data, the MetaCenter has worked a great deal on problems of storage technologies, with the greatest progress in software. The creation of a universal file format standard, a national file system with a single name space, and multivendor archiving software are some of the results of MetaCenter innovation and collaboration.

NSFNET and Networking

The 56-Kbps connection between the NSF supercomputer centers, established in 1986, was the beginning of the NSFNET. Based on the successful ARPANET and the TCP/IP protocol, the NSFNET rapidly grew to provide remote access to the NSF supercomputer centers by the creation of regional and campus connections to the backbone.

Although started by the pull from the high end, the NSFNET soon began to provide ubiquitous connectivity to the academic research community for electronic mail, file transport, and remote log-in, as well as supercomputer connectivity. As a result, the NSFNET backbone of 1995 has 3,000 times the bandwidth of the backbone of 1986. The centers have also developed prototypes for the high-performance local area networks that are needed to feed into the national backbone as well as the next generation of gigabit backbones.

Visualization and Virtual Reality

The NSF centers were instrumental in bringing the concepts and tools of scientific visualization to the research community in the 1980s. Center members developed new approaches to understanding large datasets, such as a three-dimensional grid of wind velocities and direction in a thunderstorm, by "visualizing" or creating an image from the data. This led scientists to consider visualization as an integral part of their computational tool kit. In addition, the centers worked closely with the preexisting computer graphics community, encouraging them to create new tools for scientists as well as for entertainment.

Desktop Software, Connectivity, and Collaboration Tools

The history of the centers has overlapped greatly with the worldwide rise of the personal computer and workstation. It is, therefore, not surprising that software developers focused on creating easy-to-use software tools for desktop machines. These tools have had a major influence on the usefulness of supercomputer facilities to remotely located scientists and engineers, as have tools such as NCSA's telnet, which brought full TCP connectivity to researchers using IBM and Macintosh systems, significantly broadening the base of participation beyond UNIX users. Collaboration tools have provided the capability to carry on remote digital conferencing sessions between researchers. Both synchronous and asynchronous approaches have been explored.

Development of the nation's information infrastructure requires many software, computing, and communications resources that were not traditionally thought to be part of high-performance computing. In particular, tools need to be developed for organizing, locating, and navigating through information, a task that the NSF center staffs and their associated universities continue to address. Perhaps the most spectacular success has been the NCSA Mosaic, which in less than 18 months has become the Internet "browser of choice" for over a million users and has set off an exponential growth in the number of decentralized information providers. Monthly download rates from the NCSA site alone are consistently over 70,000.

ACCOMPLISHMENTS IN EDUCATION AND OUTREACH

Each of the supercomputer centers has developed educational and outreach programs targeted to a variety of constituencies: university researchers, graduate students, undergraduates, educators at all levels, and K-12 students and teachers. Another aspect of outreach is the effort to identify and serve local and regional needs of government, schools, and communities. Activities range from the tours given at all MetaCenter installations through the hosting of visits by national, regional, and local officials and commissions, to full-scale partnerships. Table E.3 summarizes participation in these various activities.

TABLE E.3 Supercomputer Centers' Educational Activity Support Summary

Educational Activities	FY 1991	FY 1992	FY 1993
High school/K-12—Attendees	715	1,370	1,985
Research institutes—Attendees	262	377	390
Training courses and workshops—Attendees	1,700	2,400	2,100
Monthly newsletter circulation	234,986	247,692	165,176
Visitors	13,506	16,380	16,392

Researchers and Students

One- or two-day workshops offered by MetaCenter staff to researchers on-site and at associated institutions cover introductions to the computational environments, scientific visualization, and the optimization and parallelization of scientific code. In addition, special workshops have been offered throughout the MetaCenter on the use and extension of computational and visualization techniques specific to various disciplines.

MetaCenter institutions have contributed to the research projects of hundreds of graduate students through the provision of fellowships or similar appointments, stipends, access to resources, and relationships with MetaCenter researchers. Programs providing research experiences for undergraduates bring in students to work for a summer or a school semester or quarter on specific projects devised by MetaCenter researchers and/or faculty advisors. In many instances such projects have resulted in presentations at meetings and publications.

K-12 Educators and Students

Training of high school teachers and curriculum development are among the many MetaCenter educational efforts. Several programs have been initiated, such as ChemViz to help students understand abstract chemistry concepts; a visualization workshop at *Supercomputing '93*; and SuperQuest, a program involving MetaCenter sites that brings teams of teachers and students from selected high schools to summer institutes to develop computational and visualization projects that they then work on throughout the following year.

Broad Outreach

Outreach is also accomplished by the publications programs of the MetaCenter, the production of scientific videos and/or multimedia CD-ROMs, and a collaborative program for maintaining a lively and informative presence on World Wide Web servers, which make information on the MetaCenter's programs easily accessible over the nation's information infrastructure.

A number of interactive simulation programs are now being tested in classrooms across the country and around the world. Students can change initial conditions and watch a simulation evolve as the parameter space is explored. The educational programs of the MetaCenter made available to high schools around the country demonstrate the power of the nation's information infrastructure to provide new educational resources.

SCIENTIFIC COMPUTATION AND INDUSTRIAL DEVELOPMENT

Partnerships between the MetaCenter and industry are collaborations with major and large industrial firms, as well as small companies and venture start-ups. Most of these partnerships exist because MetaCenter expertise has been essential to the introduction of new ways of using the resources of supercomputing: the algorithms, visualization routines, and engineering codes are being combined in ways that result in such advances as high-end rapid prototyping of new products.

Commercialization of the software developed at the MetaCenter is being undertaken by a number of companies. For example, NCSA telnet has been commercialized by Intercon, and Spyglass has commercialized NCSA desktop imaging tools, as well as its Mosaic program. CERFnet, a California wide area network for Internet access, has pioneered in supplying access to library holdings and other large databases, and DISCOS/UniTree, a mass storage system, is in use at more than 20 major computer sites. A new molecular modeling system, called Sculpt, developed at the San Diego Supercomputing Center, is being commercialized by a new company, Interactive Simulations. Sculpt enables "drag-and-drop" molecular modeling in real time while preserving minimum-energy constraints; its output was featured on a May 1994 cover of *Science*.

IMPORTANT SCIENCE AND ENGINEERING ACCOMPLISHMENTS

Selected areas and problems, summarized below, indicate the range of projects currently being undertaken by nearly 8,000 researchers at over 200 universities and dozens of corporations and the span of disciplines now using this new tool.

Quantum Physics and Materials Science

The great disparity between nuclear, atomic, or molecular scales and macroscopic material scales implies that vast computing resources are needed to attempt to predict the characteristics of bulk matter from fundamental laws of physics. Since the beginning of the NSF centers program, researchers in this area have been among the most frequent users of supercomputers. Materials scientists have often been among the first to try out new architectures that promise higher computational speeds.

Listed below are some examples of research areas important to the study of properties of bulk matter in extreme conditions, such as occur in nuclear collisions, the early universe, or the core of Jupiter; new materials such as nanotubes and high-temperature superconductors; and more practical materials used today such as magnetic material and glass.

- Phase transitions in quantum chromodynamics
- Phase transitions of solid hydrogen
- New nanomaterials predictions

- Theory of high-temperature superconductors
- Magnetic materials

Biology and Medicine

Living creatures exhibit some of the greatest complexity found in nature. Therefore, supercomputers have made possible unprecedented opportunities to explore these complexities based on the fundamental advances made in biological research of the last 50 years. These activities include using the data from x-ray crystallography to study the molecular structure of macromolecules; learning how to use artificial intelligence to fold polypeptide chains, determined from genetic sequencing, into three-dimensional proteins; and determining the function of proteins by studying their dynamic properties.

New fields of computational science, such as molecular neuroscience, are being enabled by academic access to MetaCenter computing and visualization resources and staff. Corporations are using supercomputers and advanced visualization techniques in collaboration with the NSF MetaCenter to create new drugs to fight human diseases such as asthma. New insights into economically valuable bioproducts are being gained, for instance, by combining molecular and medical imaging techniques to create "virtual spiders" that can be dissected digitally to understand the production of silk. Finally, high-performance computers are becoming powerful enough to enable researchers to program mathematical models of realistic organ dynamics, such as the human heart. Examples of projects include the following:

- Crystallography
- Artificial intelligence and protein folding
- Protein kinase solution
- Molecular neuroscience—serotonin
- Molecular neuroscience—acetylcholinesterase
- Kinking DNA
- Antibody-antigen docking
- Tuning biomolecules to fight asthma
- Virtual spiders and artificial silk

Engineering

Man-made devices have become so complex that researchers in both academia and industry have turned to supercomputers in order to be able to analyze and modify accurate models in ways that complement traditional experimental methods. High-performance computers enable academic engineers to study the brittleness of new types of steel, improve bone transplants, or reduce the drag of flows over surfaces using riblets. Industrial partners of the individual supercomputer centers within the MetaCenter are using advanced computational facilities to improve industrial processes such as in metal forming. Better consumer products, such as leakproof diapers or more efficient airplanes, are being designed. Even state agencies are able to use the MetaCenter facilities to improve traffic safety or find better ways to use recycled materials. Some 70 corporations have taken advantage of the MetaCenter industrial programs to improve their competitiveness.

Examples of engineering-related problems include the following:

- Heart modeling
- Ultrahigh-strength steels

- Continuous casting of steel
- Beverage-can design
- Designing a leakproof diaper
- Bone transplant bioengineering
- Improving performance with riblets
- Designing better aircraft
- Crash-testing street signs

Earth Sciences and the Environment

The resources of the NSF MetaCenter are being used to compute and visualize the complexity of the natural world around us, from the motions of Earth's convective mantle to air pollution levels in southern California. The U.S. Army is working with academics to determine how to practice tank maneuvers without endangering the breeding habits of the sage grouse. Pollution is a difficult coupling of chemical reactions and flow dynamics that must be understood in detail if corrective measures are to be efficacious. High-performance computers also act as time machines, allowing for faster-than-real-time computation of severe storms. Finally, to improve global weather or climate forecasts, supercomputers allow researchers to study the physics of such critical processes as mixing at the air-ocean interface. Among the related problems being addressed are the following:

- Detoxification of ground water
- Storm modeling and forecasting
- Los Angeles smog
- Upper-ocean mixing
- Simulating climate using distributed supercomputers

Planetary Sciences, Astronomy, and Cosmology

As was evident in the recent impact of Comet Shoemaker-Levy 9 with Jupiter, observatories on Earth and in space have become intimately linked. Supercomputers are being integrated into observational facilities, like the Grand Challenge Berkeley Illinois Maryland Association millimeter observatory, and into observational programs such as the ones that have led to the discovery of new millisecond pulsars or the first extrasolar-system planet.

The ability of numerical methods to solve even the most complex of fundamental physical laws, such as Einstein's equations of general relativity, is increasing understanding of the dynamics of strong-field events, such as the collision of black holes. In perhaps the grandest-scale challenge possible, the universe itself is a subject of investigation by several Grand Challenge teams using resources of the MetaCenter to discover how the large-scale structures in the universe evolved from nearly perfect homogeneity at the time of the formation of the microwave background.

- Comet collision with Jupiter
- Discovery of first extrasolar system planet
- Pulsar searching and discovery
- Black hole collision dynamics
- Cosmological simulations

F
Individuals Providing Briefings to the Committee

Duane Adams
Advanced Research Projects Agency

William Andahazy
House Armed Services Committee

Dan Anderson
Ford Motor Company

Forest Baskett
Silicon Graphics Inc.

Gordon Bell
Computer science consultant

James Burrows
National Institute of Standards and Technology

John Cavallini
Department of Energy

Melvyn Ciment
National Science Foundation

George Cotter
National Security Agency

Craig Davis
Ford Motor Company

Hassan A. Dayem
Los Alamos National Laboratory

John deFerrari
General Accounting Office

Howard Frank
Advanced Research Projects Agency

Norm Gjostein
Ford Motor Company

Wayne Hamann
Ford Motor Company

Peter Highnam
Schlumberger Austin Research Inc.

Lee Holcomb
National Aeronautics and Space Administration

Kenneth Huebner
Ford Motor Company

Elizabeth Johnston
General Accounting Office

Anita Jones
Department of Defense

Thomas Kalil
National Economic Council

Donald Lindberg
National Library of Medicine and National Coordination Office

Ed McGaffigan
Office of U.S. Senator Jeff Bingaman

Michael Nelson
Executive Office of the President

Steve Nelson
Cray Research Inc.

Merrill Patrick
National Science Foundation

Richard Radtke
Ford Motor Company

Justin Rattner
Intel Supercomputer Systems Division

Victor H. Reis
U.S. Department of Energy

Guy L. Steele, Jr.
Thinking Machines Corporation

Paul Strassmann
Independent consultant/writer

Sing Tang
Ford Motor Company

John Toole
Advanced Research Projects Agency

Steven J. Wallach
CONVEX Computer Corporation

Philip Webre
Congressional Budget Office

James Wilson
House Science, Space, and Technology Committee

Charles Wu
Ford Motor Company